MW00615910

Now What?

© 2012 Tom Meyer

NOW WHAT?

A PRACTICAL GUIDE FOR NEWLY ELECTED OFFICIALS

LARRY TRAMUTOLA

Copyright © 2013 by Larry Tramutola.

Mill City Press, Inc.
212 3rd Avenue North, Suite 290
Minneapolis, MN 55401
612.455.2294
www.millcitypublishing.com

All rights reserved. No part of this publication may be reproduced,
stored in a retrieval system, or transmitted, in any form or by any means,
electronic, mechanical, photocopying, recording, or otherwise, without
the prior written permission of the author.

ISBN-13: 978-1-935204-86-2
LCCN: 2013902042

Cover Design by James Arneson
Typeset by Steve Porter

Printed in the United States of America

Table of Contents

Author's notes and acknowledgments

For the past forty years, I have had the pleasure (and sometimes frustration) of working with thousands of local elected officials, managing campaigns for mayors, county supervisors, city council members, judges, and school board members. I've worked with elected officials to pass local tax measures to improve public facilities, transportation, healthcare, and public safety, and I've also conducted seminars and training for elected officials in every type of public agency. I've consulted with and worked with elected officials in some of the largest and some of the smallest communities in the nation.

Despite differing abilities, background, and interests, virtually everyone elected to office goes through a steep learning curve that can seem overwhelming when first elected. Even the most committed and well-intended elected office holders struggle through their first term. Many admit privately that when they were first elected, they were ill prepared for the demands of office.

A year after being elected, a former client told me that she was frustrated and overwhelmed with the challenges of elective office. Although she was intelligent, was hardworking, and had been a very good candidate, she confided to me, "I had no idea what I was getting into. Somebody ought to write a practical guide about what it is like to go from candidate to elected official."

That conversation started me on a path to see what resources existed that could help her and other office holders in assuming the tremendous responsibility associated with the position. The more I looked, the more I was disappointed. While there are hundreds, if not thousands, of books and articles providing advice on how to get elected, there is relatively little information about being effective once elected.

Organizations like the League of Cities, the School Boards Association, and the Institute for Local Government conduct excellent training for elected officials, and these organizations publish informative guides with titles like "Understanding the Basics of County and City Revenues" or "Selecting a Conflict Resolution Professional for Inter-Agency Disputes." However, the information can be dense, overly sanitized, and often lacking in practical insights.

I realized that there was a need for something more. So I decided to interview elected officials and the people who work with them on a daily basis to see if there were common experiences that could be helpful to others.

To get a broad cross section of information and perspectives, I interviewed elected officials and staff at every level of local government. I sent surveys to current and former elected representatives and followed up with many of them who had interesting perspectives to contribute. I scoured the Internet for insight from average people to elected officials who blogged about their ideas and frustrations. I interviewed city managers, superintendents of schools, and other key managers who, ironically, are hired by elected officials, but then are expected to train and mentor the same elected officials who hired them. Reporters who cover local government also offered key insights. Finally, I studied materials put out by organizations whose mission is to foster good local government.

In my research, I was surprised how many elected officials expressed doubts and frustrations about their own effectiveness. They talked about the lack of support, training, mentoring, and feedback they received, saying they came into office ill-equipped for the job they were elected to do. They want to do a good job and they are looking for something straightforward and easy to read that could help them think through professional and personal conflicts they are facing. City managers and superintendents want a guide they can use to help them transition newly elected representatives from being candidates to effective members of an elected board.

Now What? isn't intended to be "The Idiot's Guide to Elected Office." That would be a bigger challenge. (Years ago I used one of the first "Idiot's Guides," *How to Keep Your Volkswagen Alive, A Manual of Step by Step Procedures for the Compleat Idiot* by John Muir, to repair my VW van. I followed the instructions, and even without much mechanical skill, I kept the van running.) Sadly, a step-by-step manual for being effective in elected office does not exist. Taking my hammer and hitting the solenoid a few times got my Volkswagen van running on cold days, but I wouldn't recommend the hammer approach on elected officials.

This book is written for *local* elected officials, for it is at the *local* level where most of us interact with government—through services like police, fire, and 911 calls, zoning rules and regulations, public schools, street cleaning, parks, libraries, hospitals, and community colleges, and through paying local taxes, fees, and fines.

The people who choose to serve the public at the local level are critical to well-functioning and healthy communities and to our democracy. The quality of our communities and our system of government depends on quality people running for and getting elected to these offices and being effective once they get elected.

The goal of this book is to inspire, challenge, and offer some practical advice to people elected to local office. Effective leaders can make a huge difference in their communities. Conversely, people elected to public office who are ill prepared or ineffective can create significant long-term problems.

I have eliminated the names of most elected officials, although a few remain if the stories have been written about previously. The point of this book is not to showcase individuals but to uncover common problems and practical solutions. Since we rarely elect "perfect leaders," our democratic system is structured so that ordinary citizens can be successful, if they work at it. The examples may vary, but the lessons are universal.

This book, then, is a compilation of many people's ideas, perspectives, and experiences. I'm indebted to all of them. A few individuals stood out in their insights and suggestions, however; I couldn't have written it without their sage advice. Leon Page, an attorney and community activist in San Diego, provided key observations and thoughtful reflections. Fred Brill, Lafayette superintendent and author, painstakingly provided critical advice on structure and content. Polk Laffoon IV provided thoughtful edits with the practiced eye of a former newspaper editor. I was also privileged to spend time talking with many elected officials, superintendents of schools, and city managers who candidly shared frustrations and insights. Ken Hampian, Martin Nichols, Cathy Millison, Rod Gould, Ken Nordoff, and Shirley Concolino all added important insights honed from long, successful careers in local government.

Padi Selwyn, Ann Appert, and Teresa Gerringer provided keen and thoughtful edits to the manuscript. June Monach was particularly helpful in getting the book ready for publication. Thanks to Debbie

Lee for her creativity and assistance on cover design and cover photographs. Special thanks also to Tom Meyer, syndicated political cartoonist, satirist, and keen observer of politics for his illustrations, friendship, and perspective. Any of the illustrations in this book may be used with Tom's permission. You can contact him at www.meyertoons.com.

I would also like to thank my wife, Ann Caponio Tramutola, whose opinions on all matters concerning elected officials are always insightful. Her comments made the work crisper and better.

Finally, I would also like to acknowledge all the elected officials I have worked with over the years. Each of them struggles with the challenges of being elected. Their frustrations, expressed to me in confidence, allowed me to gain a unique perspective of the challenges they face.

At the end of each chapter is a page for self reflection. Take the time to answer the questions and to think about your answers. Use the book as a notebook. Make your own lists or add to the ones we have. Take notes. Write in the book. Add your own lessons and thoughts.

To be effective in office will take hard work, dedicated study, and some introspection. Our hope is that this book will help you become a better public servant. Good luck!

Larry Tramutola
Tramutola|Advisors
TOLA (The Organizing and Leadership Academy)
Oakland, California

CHAPTER ONE
Local office, a chance to make a difference

© 2012 Tom Meyer

"We cannot become what we need
by remaining what we are."

John C. Maxwell, author

Legend has it that when Benjamin Franklin left Independence Hall in Philadelphia just after helping to write the United States Constitution in 1787, he was approached by a woman who asked him: "What manner of government have you bequeathed us?" Franklin replied, "A republic, if you can keep it." What Franklin was cautioning is a functioning democracy requires broad, and, most importantly, continued citizen involvement in government. It is through voluntary participation, debate, and eventually compromise that democratic institutions flourish.

During Franklin's lifetime, political participation was restricted to the privileged few. Today, our democracy requires (and encourages) broad citizen involvement at all levels of government. It is not enough for citizens to vote occasionally or to be modestly aware of politics. A vigorous democracy encourages healthy competition for elected offices and needs the winners to be effective in those offices once elected.

Over half of a million people currently serve in elected offices in the United States, almost all of them in local offices. Hundreds of thousands of other citizens are appointed by elected officials to serve the public on commissions and boards. Our founding fathers, who set us on this path of democracy more than two hundred years ago, would be amazed by the number of elected officials and elected offices we have today. Even more so, they would be shocked by the influence elected officials exert over so many aspects of our lives.

Local elected officials deal with significant and far-reaching issues that touch every citizen in our country. Our streets and roads, police and fire services, schools, hospitals, garbage collection, stores where we shop, zoning, quality of our parks, housing policies, even what we pay at parking meters (and the cost of the fines we get if we fail to feed the meters!) are but a few of the things influenced by the people *we* elect.

The people that we elect to serve on these elected and appointed boards are our neighbors. They come from all walks of life and are all types of people. They are moms and dads, teachers and business owners, attorneys and farmers. They are Democrats, Republicans, and Independents. They often are elected without any party designation. Some get paid; others don't. Few are professional office holders (meaning their primary source of income comes from their elected office). Most have jobs, and holding an elected office is in addition to their other responsibilities.

State and federal office holders are the most visible examples of elected officials, but they represent a tiny fraction of elected officials nationally. The vast majority of the more than 500,000 people elected to office in our country serve at the local or municipal level.

Local elected officials rarely make the national news or get interviewed on CNN. Their work might not even get reported on the inside section of the local weekly newspaper or the local political blogs. But the work that people do in local elective offices often has more impact and significance than the work of their counterparts in "higher" office. The quality of local schools is likely to be affected more by decisions made at the local level than at the national level.

Decisions of local elected officials may create more jobs than national programs. Candidates for national office may talk about "getting tough on crime," but it is at the local level where "solving crime" really happens, police are funded, neighborhood watch programs are established, and services are provided.

Because people are more likely to volunteer close to home and with people they know, local elected officials are in a great position to inspire and encourage others to become involved in community activities. Through volunteering and participating in community programs, people learn about the importance of civic engagement and participation. People you inspire to get involved may even eventually run for office, becoming the next generation of leaders.

Holding local public office is neither easy nor glamorous, but elected officials serving in local government are critical to a functioning democracy, particularly in our country where local elected representatives make significant decisions. Anyone who has traveled out of the United States knows that our system of democracy is unique. While other countries practice various forms of participatory democracy, in our country we elect citizens to serve at virtually *every* level of public life.

Elected officials have considerable influence and power, and for every person elected to office there are many others who want to be elected to those offices. Therefore, it is not surprising that electoral campaigns are highly competitive and costly. Candidates for all public offices collectively spend hundreds of millions of dollars on political campaigns, often using sophisticated communication tools to persuade voters of their "fitness" for office.

To prepare for the campaign, candidates attend seminars and training sessions to learn electoral strategies. Magazines and websites, devoted solely to elections and campaign strategy, provide advice on how to get elected. Thousands of books and articles are also available that provide guidance. In short, candidates for office have more resources and assistance and spend more money trying to get elected than ever before.

Yet, despite the money, time, and effort spent getting elected, all successful candidates have one thing in common: once elected, they will learn how to be effective on the job. Frighteningly, the people we elect to office to make our laws, decide public policy, set our tax rates, and decide how our tax dollars are spent have less training than new drivers learning to drive an automobile. While most states require successful completion of classroom instruction and usually eighteen to twenty-four hours of behind-the-wheel training, elected officials have no similar requirement to demonstrate competence or ability. There are no learners' permits or probationary periods. We elect them and hope for the best.

Elected public office is one of the few jobs where there are no significant qualifications to serve (if you exclude age and residency), there is little job training, and there are no instruction guides. There are a few, but not many, resources that help newly elected leaders become effective public servants. Our elected leaders are expected to be up and running and effective the moment they are sworn into office.

We expect our elected leaders to be effective, but their "training" takes place on the job. No successful business could operate in this manner. Through trial and error, elected officials stumble through their first few years in office, learning at the public's expense. The elected officials who take advantage of training, seminars, briefings, and mentoring are, more often than not, much more successful and happier in office. Those who don't avail themselves of these resources often become frustrated and, regrettably, less effective than they could be.

If you are one of the people elected to local office, you have a unique opportunity to help guide your community by providing leadership and intelligent decision making to difficult and complex problems. Our democracy only works if good people run for office. Serving the public, as an elected representative, is one of the most important things you will do in life. Knowing what you believe in; knowing why you ran for office; knowing what you want to accomplish in office; and honing the skills to be effective will be critical to your eventual success.

This book will take you through the steps of learning about your job, developing effective relationships with your colleagues, setting boundaries, taking the small steps that lead to big changes, and communicating effectively. It will help you avoid the pitfalls and the mistakes of others. You will learn that winning an election for public office is only the beginning. The real work starts after you are elected, and the harder you work, the better you'll be. It's all here, a step-by-step practical guide for becoming effective in local government.

Each chapter ends with a series of questions to help you organize yourself. The hope is that you'll take a few minutes to think about the lessons in each chapter. There will never be a time when you will be more inspired or optimistic than when you first get elected to office. This is the time to develop good habits. As you serve, your ideas and perspectives will change. Attending countless meetings, studying esoteric staff reports, listening to impassioned and informed people, and observing firsthand how government does and doesn't work will influence your thinking and your decision making. But now, as a newly elected leader, and before your responsibilities and workload become overwhelming, take a few moments to think about who you are and why you want to be in public office. This is your opportunity to make a difference.

Eventually you may be interested in higher office, and serving at the local level can be a great training ground. People who serve at the local level first, then go on to higher office, are more likely to be successful than those who haven't served in local office. The key, however, to move to higher office from local government, is to make an impact at the local level first. Before you run for higher office it is a good idea to be effective in the job you currently have. But we are getting ahead of ourselves. We are not talking, yet, about moving on (see chapter eighteen). Being effective at the job you have will require developing good habits, and many of the habits you learned as a candidate will be habits you'll need to break as an elected official.

© 2012 Tom Meyer

Self Reflection

What skills will you need to be an effective leader?

_____

_____

If you could accomplish just one thing in office, it would be this:

_____

_____

After your term of office is over, what would you like people to say about you? How would you like to be remembered?

_____

_____

Who in public life would you want to pattern your public life after?

_____

_____

CHAPTER TWO

The election is over. I won! Now what?

© 2012 Tom Meyer

"What do we do now?"

Senator-elect Bill McKay,

fictional character in *The Candidate*

In the 1972 movie *The Candidate*, the reluctant candidate, Bill McKay, played by Robert Redford, upon learning that he just won the U.S. Senate seat from California, utters the famous line, "What do we do now?"

Unfortunately, the movie ends with that scene and we never learn what the new senator will accomplish in his term. Since Senator McKay has no previous experience in elected office, we are left to wonder: "Will he be successful?" "Will he be effective?" "Will he sell out or burn out?"

We can only guess that Senator McKay will soon learn what thousands of other first-time elected officials eventually learn: *Running for office is a whole lot different from being in office, and there are very few resources to help you be effective.*

It shouldn't be that way, and in a few places it's not. There are, in some select communities, programs to mentor the "incoming class" of elected officials, as well as efforts to provide these elected officials with the necessary tools to help them be successful. In other communities, the city manager, the city clerk, or the superintendent of schools will make an effort to train and mentor newly elected representatives. But, it is more common that mentoring doesn't happen, and most newly elected officials do not take advantage of the few courses and orientations that are offered. As a result, elected officials are usually on their own to figure things out.

With rare exception, the people elected to our city councils, school and community college boards, hospital boards, water districts, and boards of supervisors want to do a good job. Moreover, it is not as though they deal with mundane or unimportant issues where experience or training is not important. These ordinary people who are elected to solve extraordinary problems often have little idea of how to be effective. Given that, it's ironic that they receive so little on-the-job training.

Their one qualification is they were elected. People go from "candidate" one day to "leader" the next without proper training or skills.

Gary Neely, a consultant to local governmental agencies, observes: "Whatever elected officials thought they were getting into when they decided to run, they were wrong. Being an elected official is nothing like what they could have imagined before being elected. The higher the office, the more drastic the difference will be."

So if elected officials aren't adequately prepared for office, what do they do? It starts with a reflection upon the reasons you, the candidate, first ran for office and an understanding of what your job is.

A number of years ago, in my capacity as a political consultant, I decided that instead of being interviewed by potential candidates, I would interview them. I wanted to know what motivates the person who wants my help. I wanted to know what they care about and what they want to accomplish in office.

When I interview a prospective candidate, one of my first questions is: "Why do you want to be in office?" I'm often disappointed with the answers. Unfortunately, very few candidates have taken the time to really think about what they want to accomplish in office. Most have little idea of the difference between leading and being on a legislative body. Figuring out how to win seems more important (and maybe more exciting) than figuring out what they want to accomplish and how they will accomplish it. When asked "Why do you want to win?" or "Why do you want to be in office?" I have heard everything:

"Well, hmmm, I've always wanted to be a leader."
"I think I'd like to be in Washington (or the state house)."
"I'd like to be a senator some day, and this is a good place to start."
"My union/pastor/friends/family encouraged me to run."
"I'm a natural leader."
"I want to bring dignity to American families."
"I'll fight crime."
"There is too much waste in government."
"I believe in hope and prosperity."
"I'll create new jobs."
"I'll end the partisanship and bickering."

I've even heard the best line of all: "I ran because I wanted the health coverage!"

Over the years, I've learned that money and smart strategy can help overcome the flaws of a poor candidate. But regrettably, once they are elected, their flaws cannot be hidden. Elected officials who had no good reasons as to why they ran for office and have no clear goals can cause serious and long-term problems. Ambition is not a good enough reason to run for office.

Campaigning for office and being in office are as different as dating and being married. While one may lead to the other, the former definitely doesn't prepare you for the latter.

It is the rare candidate who has clear, well-articulated, and thoughtful ideas why he or she is running or what he or she wants to accomplish. A candidate who is able to clearly articulate why he or she wants to be elected, and what he or she wants to accomplish in office, has a better chance of being successful once in office. This is not about campaign slogans or sound bites. It requires serious self-reflection as to the reasons for wanting to be elected.

Did you have a specific reason for running for office? What specific changes do you want to make? Why? Did you run because you merely wanted to be elected, or do you have specific issues in mind that you want to work on? If you have goals, be realistic about them. You will need to be ready to work hard if you want to achieve even a fraction of what you want.

One of the most important things you will learn is that you were elected to be a policy maker, not a manager. While it is normal for newly elected officials to think they have been elected to run the bureaucracy, that's not the case. Except for mayors (the ones who actually are the CEOs of the city, not those elected to honorary positions), you have been elected to set policy, not run the bureaucracy.

You help set priorities about where money will be spent and where it won't. You don't run the public works department. You don't hire and supervise principals or teachers. You don't tell police officers how to do their jobs. Your job is to set broad policies and allocate resources so the professional staff can do the work they were hired to do. This is a good thing. It allows you to see the big picture rather than getting mired in details.

Attorney Leon Page, who works in the County Counsel office in Orange County, adds this perspective: "Candidates often miss the fact that they are seeking election to what is, in almost all cases, a *legislative body*. As members of a legislative body, their primary function is to check and balance the agency's chief executive officer, usually a hired professional manager. Local agency legislators are not managers or agency executives themselves, they are not part of the CEO's management team, and they are not members of some kitchen cabinet. They are to the CEO, city manager, or superintendent as the congress is to the president. Their job is to scrutinize administration proposals, enact local legislation, and approve a budget.

"Once the legislative role is clearly understood, everything else follows, and normal controversies can be analyzed in the proper context. As local legislators, they should look beyond any partisan or ideological differences between themselves and other council members when necessary. They'll garner more respect if they do. Councils that have the view that 'we're all in this together'—where the mayor acts like the team's coach—tend to perform better than those dominated by faction, where one group is trying to jam the other."

Before you file your papers to run for office and before you talk to one voter or raise a single dollar, it would be a good idea to develop a "to do" list of the things you want to accomplish in office. If you haven't done this already, now is your chance. Finish reading the chapter; then do your list.

Your list should be specific and include categories of goals. It should include things that require voter approval (a bond measure for facility or infrastructure improvements, for instance, or a parcel tax perhaps, or even an advisory vote on an important public policy issue). Your list should also include things that can be accomplished through leadership and working with the community. Will you need to have the support of the majority of your fellow elected colleagues, or can your goals be accomplished without legislative approval? Each goal should have a time attached as to when you believe it can be accomplished. All goals should be ranked from top to bottom, most important to least. Your goals may change once you are in office, but knowing what you want to accomplish is a good start.

When California Governor Jerry Brown ran for mayor of Oakland, he specifically said that his goal was to revitalize the downtown area. To accomplish this goal he encouraged housing construction that brought ten thousand more residents to the downtown. As mayor, Brown held himself and his administration accountable for achieving that goal. Brown knew that if he wanted to provide better services he had to increase revenue in the city.

After eight years as mayor, Jerry Brown was recognized as having been effective because he had a clear goal, knew what he wanted to accomplish, articulated that vision to voters, and then, most importantly, made it a priority in everything he did once in office. The city staff followed his lead, and downtown Oakland today is now experiencing a renaissance in retail and housing because Mayor Brown knew what he wanted to accomplish and kept at it day after day. His successors, on the other hand, have had difficulties, because they either had no specific attainable goals or they did not make accomplishing them a priority.

Being a local elected official can be tough. It will take a tremendous amount of time, effort, discipline, and compromise to accomplish even modest goals. Most local elected officials get paid very little (usually) to make difficult decisions. The decisions you make can cause you to lose, not win, friends. If you don't know why you are doing it, or what you want to accomplish, or if you lack commitment, you will not be successful.

So take some time to think through what you want to accomplish.

Self Reflection

Why did you want to be elected? (If your list sounds corny or too general, it probably is. Try again).

_____

_____

What new skills do you need to acquire to be effective in office?

_____

_____

Where will you learn these things? What training is available?

_____

_____

Finally, list the things you want to accomplish in office. Be as specific as possible. Write down the dates when you want to accomplish these goals. Prioritize your goals.

CHAPTER THREE

Being effective takes work, a lot of it

"My grandfather once told me that there were two kinds of people: those who do the work and those who take the credit. He told me to try to be in the first group; there was much less competition."

Indira Gandhi (1917–1984), Prime Minister of India

Going through the steps of successfully running for office, being elected, and then serving is similar to the process of applying for college, getting accepted, and then being in college. To be accepted to the college of your choice took effort. You needed to take the right courses in high school and do well in them; you needed to be involved in activities outside of the classroom; and you needed to prepare a quality personal statement that highlighted your abilities, background, and potential. Perhaps you even had a personal interview. This, plus luck (and perhaps connections), got you accepted.

Once you got accepted to college none of that mattered anymore. Your success in college rested on your willingness and motivation to study, work hard, and learn from others. Your success as an elected official, like being successful in college, also rests on your willingness and motivation to study, work hard, and learn from others.

As a candidate, you worked hard to be accepted by voters. You were involved in the community. You prepared your personal statement of qualifications highlighting your abilities and background. You were interviewed many times during your campaign. None of this will have much to do with your effectiveness as an elected leader.

It is a rare person who is successful in college that doesn't work hard, and it is the rare elected official who will be successful without continued hard work and continued learning. Few elected officials are effective immediately. Problems are likely to be a lot more complex than you thought as a candidate, and your fellow colleagues may not share your views.

Martin J. Nichols, former city manager of the City of Red Bluff, California, provides some practical advice for all newly elected officials. His list is smart and succinct and should be required reading for every newly elected person. (I wish I had thought up the list!) His words are in italics, mine in regular type.

*1. **Learn the rules of the game.** Both the League [of California Cities] and CSAC [California State Association of Counties and others] have new council member/supervisor trainings. Plan to attend. Your first few months will be spent absorbing a lot of information and knowledge on how the agency works. Attend a training session six months or a year after you are first elected. You will have a better appreciation of what you need to know.*

City Manager Nichols is referring to resources in California, but in most states there are trainings sponsored by the League of Cities, the School Boards Association, the Institute for Local Government, or other similar organizations. Knowing the rules, and most importantly, learning what you don't know, will give you an appreciation for your new job and get you off on the right foot.

Learn everything you can about the job *before* taking office. Get copies of old board minutes and look at relevant newspaper articles. Talk to current and past elected officials. What advice do they have?

Rod Gould, Santa Monica's city manager, encourages elected officials to also become involved with regional and statewide organizations to gain perspective and to leverage their own agency's influence. This experience adds to the effectiveness of the elected official. "The best elected officials have a sense of what is going on in the region and statewide and have networks of other officials to call upon for advice and support."

*2. **Work with management.** The city manager and county administrator have a vested interest in getting the new member up to speed. They are experienced in translating "government speak" into concepts that the new member can grasp. Meet with them before each meeting to review the agenda until you are comfortable with the subject matter. Get clear with the chief executive on his/her expectations for meeting with subordinate staff.*

Meeting regularly with the chief executive is also true for school board members (who need to work with the superintendent) and elected officials in other agencies that have a hired chief executive. Most non-elected leaders (city managers, school superintendents, hospital administrators, etc.) say they want more individual time with elected leaders, not less. Building a good relationship with each person on the management team of your public agency is extremely important. The work of these people will determine your success in office.

The smart city manager (superintendent or general manager) will offer orientations for new officials as soon as they are elected. This will give the elected official insight into the inner workings of the agency and help them avoid making missteps or come in guns-a-blazing, but unable to accomplish anything. If you haven't been given a thorough orientation, demand that you get one.

City Manager Nichols emphasizes: "A good staff will also provide highly structured goal setting/work program development processes in order to establish collective council-board priorities. And they will design systems to integrate priorities within employee and organizational work programs (so that elected officials know that these processes have real 'juice' and are worth the effort). A good city manager will also motivate elected officials to participate in formal team-building workshops among themselves and with staff, get them to conferences, etc."

3. Pick a mentor. *Follow the lead of a member of the governing board you trust and respect for the first few meetings until you learn the issues.*

Your fellow elected colleagues, whether you like them or not, may have a lot of experience and knowledge. Is there one you feel you can learn from? Ask that person in private about an issue you need guidance on. If no one in the current board can help, is there a former board member who can mentor you? You have now become part of a team, and you need to work cooperatively. Acknowledge you do not know everything. Effective boards often have one or more individuals who take a special interest in a specific area of policy. Have you determined what your specific interest is? Have you identified someone who can mentor you?

4. Rhetoric to reality. *Recognize that the issues facing your organization are a lot more complex than you imagined. If they were easily solved, they wouldn't still be issues. Plan on getting grounded in your high-priority issues before offering action plans. Avoid the embarrassment and frustration of offering "solutions" that can't be implemented. Avoid getting pinned down on issues before you* *understand the views of all parties. Have a set of guiding principles to fall back on in complex matters. Try to avoid getting buried in the details.*

The thorny, difficult problems you thought (or promised) you could solve when you were a candidate will invariably prove to be a lot tougher once you're in office. Don't be afraid to ask lots of questions. Ask them of your colleagues, the staff, and department heads. Asking questions will allow you to hear different perspectives. It also shows you care and are willing to listen. No one expects you to know very much at this point, so this is a good time to learn as much as you can.

Despite the rhetoric used in campaigns ("I'll make change," "I'll get pensions under control," "I'll eliminate waste"), it is unlikely that as an individual member of a board you will be able to accomplish much very quickly or by yourself. Issues are always more complex than you thought before you were elected. Take the time to learn before you push for new policies or actions.

5. Meet with each department head. *Meet with each department head to discuss the issues facing the department and those you can expect to be brought to the council/board in the next year. Visit the facilities—see the issues—"a picture is worth a thousand words." Pace yourself—one department a week–so learning occurs.*

Voting on the issues that come before you is a small part of the job. The real work is done behind the scenes where you really learn how your agency functions. While you are not running departments, you are setting policy, and the more you know about each department, the easier it will be to react when issues come before you. In many ways, you need to be a student of all the inner workings of your agency so you can set policy. Poke around. If you are on a school board, visit the schools. If you are a city council member, visit fire stations, police stations, the public works department, and organizations and programs that receive funding.

Part of governance is balancing limited resources. How does one department stack up against another? Are there areas where the bureaucracy seems bloated or where services are duplicated? Just because a program provides a public service doesn't mean it is effective or efficient. A goal may be to streamline government, but what will be the impact of cutting programs or services? The more you learn, the better your chances of developing good policies.

6. Meet the other players. *Meet with the other members of the council/board individually to get their take on how the governing board works together, their priorities for issues facing the agency, how they expect to be dealt with on public issues, and to clarify any misconceptions they might have about you. Remember, nothing important to you happens unless two other members agree with you in a public meeting (the "count to three rule"). You should also meet governing board members of other public agencies important to the mission of your organization. You will also need to meet union leaders, issue advocacy groups, and business leaders.*

One of the most important things you will have to deal with is balancing the needs/wants of the insiders (those who know the inner workings of your agency and who are passionate advocates for their positions) with the needs of the average person (who has little interest in the affairs of the agency). Insiders can dominate decision making, and the average citizen is either too busy to get involved or doesn't know how to get his or her voice heard.

Elected officials are surrounded by insiders. You need to make sure that it is not just the insiders that have your ear. This is not easy. You will always hear the views of those who are most passionate, but the interests of the most passionate may not be in the best interest of the broader public. Perhaps you were supported by various interest groups during your election, but as an elected official you have a responsibility for the entire community. Many people feel the crisis with public employee pension plans could have been avoided if the people who will eventually foot the bill had been at the table during negotiations. Who speaks for the public? Who represents the larger community? You do.

Keep in mind that you were elected to serve all the people, not just those who voted for you, and definitely not those who yell the loudest, may threaten, are the most influential, or can pack a meeting.

7. Give yourself time. *Plan on being lost for six months, understanding most issues at one year, and knowing what needs to be done—at eighteen months.*

Being lost for six months does not mean being inactive. It takes months, if not longer, to learn a new language. Becoming proficient at anything takes time. Give yourself the time. Don't worry about being graded on your first hundred days or even your first year in office.

Spend your time learning, asking questions, and developing your long-term plan. If you haven't attended a training session in your first year, however, something is wrong. Make sure you are learning about your office. Most terms of office are four years and most elected officials serve at least two terms. You have a long time to make a difference. Use your "honeymoon" to learn.

8. Throw away paper. *Toss (recycle) most of what you are given. Staff has copies if you need them.*

You can get buried in detail and paper. The amount of paper you will be given, even in small agencies, can be overwhelming. Scan what you need and recycle the rest. Determine what level of detail you need. Your job is to see the big picture and not get bogged down in minutia.

9. Find work–life balance. *Staff and constituents will keep you busy 24/7 if you let them.*

We devote a full chapter (thirteen) to setting limits. Official responsibilities and meetings can consume all of your life if you allow them to. Suffice it to say that having balance in life is critical to being effective, yet it takes work to achieve it. Without balance, marriages suffer, children are neglected, and an elected official may become stale and jaded. While elected office can be time consuming, at times difficult, and occasionally stressful, it should not negatively affect your health or your family.

Try to develop interests outside of your elected office. You will enjoy your work more and you will be more effective if you have interests other than your political or elected life. Saying "no" to meetings or special events will allow you to focus on your goals. You don't need to be accountable twenty-four hours a day.

10. Trust your instincts. *You will never be the expert in all the things you need to decide. Learn to rely on that inner voice on who to trust/believe on various issues. It was those instincts that got you elected.*

Instincts are gained from experience and repetition. Don't expect to have all the answers. You are likely, at times, to feel overwhelmed and not up to the task. That's common and healthy. Read, study, ask, and listen. Think long-term. Think about how the decision you are making today may play out a year from now or ten years from now. You will make mistakes. Learn from them and move on. Do what is right—forget the political ramifications.

A city council member told me: "I was completely lost my first year in office. Being in this role is a lot harder than I anticipated. I had always been successful in everything I tried, but elected office was somewhat overwhelming. The first thing I had to learn was that I needed to be a student again. Reading, studying, listening—skills I learned in school were the same skills I needed as an elected official."

Joyce Starosciak, a former city council member in San Leandro, California, described her learning this way: "I worked hard to get to where I am, but I have to continually work to keep up with new information. Being a council member is a lot harder than people think. I'm pretty smart, but I just can't show up to a meeting and think it is enough. I also ask my close friends and family to make sure I don't become totally absorbed in the job. I always remind myself that I am part of a continuum of elected officials that came before me and will come after me. I am not indispensable. I just try to do my best and do what is right. It is not always easy."

Self Reflection

Have you signed up for training and orientation sessions?

_____

_____

Have you established a regular one-on-one meeting with your agency's CEO and department heads?

_____

_____

Who could be a mentor to you? Why is he/she the best choice?

_____

_____

What strategies do you have so you don't become dominated by insiders?

_____

_____

Look at every request of your time. What can be eliminated?

_____

_____

CHAPTER FOUR

Working with colleagues

© 2012 Tom Meyer

"The leaders who work most effectively . . . never say 'I.' And that's not because they have trained themselves not to say 'I.' They don't think 'I.' They think 'we'; they think 'team.' They understand their job [is] to make the team function. They accept responsibility and don't sidestep it, but 'we' gets the credit. This is what creates trust, what enables you to get the task done."

Peter F. Drucker, author and management consultant

When you are a candidate for office, everything you do is about *you*. What *you* are going to do once *you* are elected. What skills and qualifications *you* have. Who endorsed *you*. Why *you* will be better than your opponent.

Once *you* are elected you quickly learn that nothing is accomplished alone. You will need the support of the majority of the elected board on which you sit to accomplish your goals. If there are seven members, you will need four votes to get anything done. If there are five, you will need two others (the Rule of Three). You have been elected to be part of a team, whether you want to be or not.

Policies, budgets, and hiring decisions will be decided by the majority. If you are not able to work with the majority and be part of the majority, your term in office will be frustrating, and it will be impossible to accomplish very much. Establishing and maintaining good working relationships with your colleagues will take effort, patience, and diplomacy. Your success rests on it.

Once again, the League of Cities, the Institute for Local Government, and the School Boards Association provide training and seminars on developing collaborative relations with your elected colleagues. Their seminars are well worth attending. Learning how to engage in joint goal setting and how to avoid conflicts with your colleagues are essential skills. Study sessions, even retreats, can help build understanding and cooperation among board members.

Building good working relationships with your fellow elected leaders will take a great deal of effort and patience, as not all of your colleagues will share your values or goals. Some may make decisions that are not in the interest of the public. You may even privately wonder how some of your colleagues ever got elected in the first place or how they got re-elected. Some are lazy, some don't seem very smart, and some just go through the motions. Even worse, some make decisions to benefit their own interests or special interests.

But like them or not, effective or not, the public expects you to get along with your colleagues, and more importantly, to get things done. If you are elected to a board where there is no drama, no controversies, where your fellow members work together cooperatively, consider yourself lucky.

The public has, unfortunately, become accustomed to partisan quarreling and one-upmanship at the state and federal level where neither political party is willing or able to compromise. But at the local level, the public wants civility and expects that local elected officials will work together to solve problems. To achieve this goal, you need to avoid petty quarrels. You don't have to win every argument or every vote.

John Nalbandian, a former elected official who now teaches at the University of Kansas, says that the most important constituents of an elected official are the other council members. Nothing, he observes, gets done without a majority. Nalbandian provides some insightful tips for local elected officials: His comments are in italics, mine in regular type.

- *Compromise and negotiation are the tools of the political craft. Except when sitting as a quasi-judicial body, beware of acting like judge and jury. You are a member of a legislative body where compromise and negotiation are prized.*

Unfortunately, not everyone values compromise or recognizes that compromise is the only way to make progress. Some view compromise as selling out or giving up. It's not. Half steps are sometimes the only way to move forward. As an elected official you will rarely get everything you want. The truly successful elected officials are those that learn the art of compromise.

- *Working with other council members to accomplish something is incredibly rewarding. But it may mean giving up some of what you want. Keep your focus on what you are trying to accomplish. The emotions of politics and dealing with citizens can take you off track.*

It will be necessary at times to disagree with your supporters and your constituents. This is not easy. You have to develop the ability to think independently. You develop this skill by listening to others and by acting calmly when emotion is high. Good decisions are rarely made playing to the crowd or when emotions are high.

- *Your toughest job initially will be learning how to get other council members to consider "your" issues. There are formal ways to get items on the governing body's agenda, and there are informal ways to interest other council members.*

Meeting individually with the chief executive and with your fellow colleagues will provide opportunities to see if there is support for what you want to do. Doing this work, quietly and behind the scenes, can save time and embarrassment.

- *Learn how to engage your colleagues without enraging them.*

Treating each colleague (even those with whom you disagree) with respect is essential. You gain nothing if you are disrespectful. Body language including rolling your eyes, not paying attention when others are talking, shaking your head, or leaving the meeting can be more damaging than words. Your colleagues deserve respect and attention.

- *Sometimes you have to be satisfied just to have the governing body consider an issue you are interested in. You will not always get your way.*

Just raising an issue sometimes is important. You may be in the minority, but having discussion and debate may be an important step.

- *For the sake of effective meetings, every council member does not have to speak on every issue.*

Chapter seven is devoted to this point. Countless hours of time are wasted when elected officials feel a need to speak on every issue.

Newly elected members of a board require mentoring and time to get up to speed. Your chief executive (city manager or superintendent, for example) can be a valuable resource. These executives have the responsibility to make sure the elected leaders have the information and context to make quality decisions. While the chief administrator is the only hired employee of the board, he or she is also a coach, a facilitator, and a trainer to the elected board.

Sometimes elected boards don't function well. Petty quarrels, jealousy, and disagreements drain time, money, and energy. If your board is not functioning well you may need to talk with your chief executive to develop trainings. Working effectively with your colleagues will require patience and cooperation.

One elected official shared her frustration: "Sure, it's fine when I limit how much I talk or if I follow the rules. The problem is my colleagues don't follow the rules. What am I to do?"

First, make sure the rules for conducting meetings and speaking are understood by all. Second, the president of the board or the council must be empowered to enforce the rules. Third, when issues emerge, meet with your colleagues privately to express your concerns.

Knowing what is important to your colleagues and understanding their motivations and perspectives will allow you to find issues you can tackle together. Is an elected colleague a former employee of the agency who has retired and thinks he knows more than anyone else? How will you deal with him? Does someone have a chip on her shoulder and won't or doesn't want to work collectively? Are you dealing with a single-issue person or the pessimist who, as Winston Churchill observed, "sees difficulty in every opportunity" and who at every meeting drains the energy out of the room? Often these people say "no" so they don't have to be responsible if something does not

34

go perfectly. Has one of your colleagues been elected by an interest group to protect their interests? Does one of your colleagues have political ambition and make decisions based on that ambition? How can your goals and her goals mesh?

A respected city manager told me, "Some elected officials are there for the wrong reasons and cannot be counted on to make good public policy. The leader should not allow these people to sabotage good policy or lead bad policy."

Recognizing the strengths and weaknesses of your colleagues is not something you will learn in seminars. Study your fellow board members. Determine what issues you can collaborate on. Recognize that there are limits to collaboration.

As one member of a team you need to find out what's important to other members. Disagreements on personnel and priorities are normal. Finding ways to work together to make progress despite these disagreements will require patience and persistence.

Your success is about *we*, not *me*!

© 2012 Tom Meyer

Self Reflection

How will I develop a good relationship with each of my colleagues?

_____

_____

How will I respond when disagreements emerge?

_____

_____

What issues are particularly important to each of my colleagues?

_____

_____

What are the most important issues we can work on together?

_____

_____

What are the implications if we fail to learn to collaborate?

CHAPTER FIVE

To get things done, control your ego

© 2012 Tom Meyer

"The great corrupter of public man is the ego. . . . Looking at the mirror distracts one's attention from the problem."

Dean Acheson, former U.S. Secretary of State

For the first-time candidate there is nothing more exhilarating than the feeling of being declared the winner on Election Day. Whether the victory was by a few votes or by a landslide, every successful candidate believes his or her election was because voters "got it." "Voters obviously understood who the better candidate was and they selected *me*!"

Every election has winners and losers. You won. You're a winner. Wow. What a feeling! People you don't even know offer their best wishes. Flower arrangements and notes of congratulations are sent from your supporters and from people who want to know you. Your name appears in the local papers listing you as a winner. It's not hard to feel damn good about yourself and to think you are pretty special.

Get over yourself. You are not that special.

Maybe your winning was a fluke. Maybe voters really didn't "get it" and you were elected because there was no one better, or maybe your opponent(s) campaigned poorly. Maybe you were just lucky. The public often votes against someone rather than for someone. Somebody had to be elected. It happened to be you.

Having spent the better part of forty years helping people get elected, I know that election results are often less about the better candidate and more about luck, resources, and timing. Voters can have a difficult time differentiating between candidates, and sometimes they make decisions that seem less than rational; sometimes they are wrong. The best people don't always get elected. Voters can make mistakes, and even if they didn't, they may have a hard time articulating why they voted for one person over another.

"I voted for the woman."

"I never vote for a woman."

"I always vote against incumbents."

"I voted for the first name listed."

"My union, my neighbor, my minister, my mother, my barber . . . told me who to vote for."

"I can't remember which one I voted for, but I'm pretty sure I voted."

You were elected because someone had to be.

Perhaps you were the best candidate. Maybe voters did make a good decision. Time will tell. Eventually you will be judged not on how well you ran your campaign, but how well you perform in office. So whether you were the best candidate or not, it really doesn't matter. You are the person who is going to get sworn in, and you are the one who will be held accountable in office.

Whether you won because of luck or you won because you were the better choice, you should assume you won because of a fluke.

Why?

Your own ego may be your biggest obstacle to being successful, and the bigger your ego, the bigger the problem.

This is so important I am going to say it again. Your own ego may be your biggest obstacle to being successful, and the bigger your ego, the bigger the problem. An inflated ego inhibits an elected official from making wise decisions. It inhibits listening and learning from others. It blocks the ability to let others share in the credit.

41

Maybe you ran a good campaign, but good campaigners do not necessarily make good elected officials. There is absolutely no correlation between running a good campaign or winning an election and being effective in office. Your goal, hopefully, was not merely to run a good campaign and win, but to be a good elected leader.

So your first challenge is to control your ego.

Brian Floyd has been around politics his entire life. His uncle was the late California Assemblyman Dick Floyd. Brian has been a student of, and been involved in, politics at the local, state, and federal levels for many years. Here is what he says: "The biggest problem I see in politics is that too many people run for office to be someone important instead of to do something important. That's why so many campaign promises go unfulfilled. The problem could easily be fixed if these folks understood that if they accomplished something important, they would be viewed as people who are important. Good policy makes for good politics. Public opinion is always shifting. Leaders need to do the right thing even under a lot of pressure."

So how does someone with a big enough ego to run for office keep his or her ego in check once elected?

1. The office you hold is more important than you.

You are now expected to have answers to a lot of complex problems. All of a sudden, people will come up to you in grocery stores or on the street and want to talk. People who never knew you existed, or cared if you did, are asking you for advice, or they are requesting a meeting that will take "just a few minutes of your time."

Remember, you are no smarter this week than you were last week; the difference is people expect you to have answers—and the ability to fix their problem. They perceive that you have power, and they want something from you. With all this attention, it is natural to feel just a little bit special, that perhaps you are smarter and that you do have the ability to solve problems.

Even if you are smart and you have some answers, think of yourself as a student from day one. You have a lot to learn and it is going to take time to accomplish what you want. Defining yourself as a student who has a lot to learn will help keep your ego in check.

Controlling your ego is not easy. Former San Francisco Mayor Art Agnos learned the hard way. Art was finishing his third year in office. I had directed his field operations during his first campaign for mayor and he was eager to duplicate our earlier success on his re-election campaign. Art had a successful first term in office and gained national attention after the Loma Prieta earthquake devastated the city. He appeared on national TV, was interviewed on major news stories, and became somewhat of a celebrity mayor. He was pumped up and ready for national politics. Some even considered him a vice presidential candidate.

Prior to getting his second campaign started, I asked a trusted group of volunteers and former campaign workers to fan out across the city into various neighborhoods and ask people which city problem "bugged them most." The answer came back loud and clear: Dirty streets was the thing that most bugged them. I suggested to Art that we make cleaning the streets our focus for a few months and that he, as mayor, his volunteers, and our campaign staff actually go out and sweep the streets in neighborhoods across the city, as a symbolic and tangible gesture. He immediately declined, telling me in no uncertain terms, "No way. Sweeping streets is beneath The Mayor." I couldn't convince him. Instead he wanted to focus on telling voters about all the great things he had accomplished in his first term.

Meanwhile, our opposition, I'm sure, had also heard what we had heard from citizens. Several weeks after the mayor had rejected our idea of sweeping, our opponent and his supporters began sweeping the streets. The press loved it. The public loved it. Even though the election was some months away, the debate had been defined. Art's opponent listened to the public and responded. Art was perceived as being aloof and more interested in telling voters what he accomplished rather than responding to what voters wanted. On Election Day, the voters swept Art Agnos out of office.

2. Don't accept perks. None of them, not even the small ones. (This can be such a problem that we have devoted a whole chapter to it!)

Free parking? Don't accept it. How are you going to understand the frustrations of people trying to find change to put in parking meters if you are able to park anywhere you want for free? Free tickets to games and events? Say no. Give those tickets to the Boys Club or the Girls Club or to the Scouts. Never use them yourself.

Is there a pothole in front of your house that you want fixed? Go through the channels like any other citizen. Resist the impulse to call the director of public works. You need to know what the average citizen goes through to get a response from government.

There was an article in the *New York Times* on July 15, 2011, by Shoshana Walter, about two elected officials who, after having their cars broken into, called the chief of police directly for action. While understandable, the average citizen has neither the relationship nor the ability to call the chief of police directly. The average citizen, who has no connections, might wait days for action if they get any response at all. Elected officials should not receive special treatment or attention merely because they are office holders.

A meal at a board meeting is not a perk, but going to a restaurant on the public's dime is. It is really not that hard to differentiate between the two. If you are getting something for free that the public isn't, it is a perk and you should turn it down. This is not about a new Puritanism. It is about keeping your ego in check and realizing that being in public office does not entitle you to free passes for trips, dinners, concerts, or ball games. We have no royalty in this country.

Special treatment and insignificant perks may seem innocuous, but it is the acceptance of the special things that you get and that others don't that messes with your ego. Why do we give presents to friends and family? To make them feel special. Elected officials do not need to feel special. While gifts and other freebies have to be reported on conflict of interest statements, it is better to never take the gifts in the first place. It's not the gift. It's what it does to your ego. By accepting gifts, even small ones, you start thinking you are special.

The public may not be aware of the gift or special treatment you may receive, but eventually people find out. Don't contribute to the perception that elected officials are out for themselves, that they receive special favors.

Read the sage advice of Leon Page, an attorney from Carlsbad, California:

"I would discourage travel junkets and expense reimbursement claims, as the temptations are too great, and bright careers are often snuffed out, not by major quid pro quo corruption, but by petty claims such as a fancy dinner or free tank of gas on the public's dime. The self-serving behavior may actually be 'small potatoes,' but the public will be able to relate to it even more."

A respected superintendent of a large school district was fired, not because of his failures at leading the district, but because he turned in his receipts for his morning coffee at Starbucks for reimbursement. Despite his hefty and generous salary, he had no problem asking taxpayers to pay for his coffee (or even worse, he didn't consider who was paying for it). Teachers, facing layoffs because of budget cuts, and parents, who saw course offerings and programs reduced, were justifiably angry. There was one set of rules for the superintendent, another for everyone else. It wasn't the money, it was the principle and the perception.

In San Diego, a superior court judge was removed from the bench because she billed taxpayers for the cost of her hotel and expenses for a three-day conference. The problem was the now ex-judge only attended a half day of the conference and spent the rest of the time sightseeing with her boyfriend.

As an elected official, you will receive advice on how to legally report gifts. Make your life simple. Don't accept them. If you have to report a gift, it's probably not a good idea to accept it in the first place.

3. Get out of the office. Walk precincts, go door to door, and walk through the business districts, even when there is no election and you don't have to.

If you are knocking on people's doors at a time when you are not asking for their vote, you will gain more than just invaluable insight and knowledge. You will also gain a lot of respect.

Going door to door is far more important than constituent meetings where people come to you. Most constituent meetings only attract the insiders. Going door to door reaches people on their terms, their homes.

By walking the neighborhoods and knocking on people's doors, you'll learn things that you would never learn in constituent meetings. You will be amazed how few people know you exist and how appreciative people are that you've taken time to drop by. Most importantly, you will learn what is on *their* minds. Listen and take notes. This is something that should be done consistently and regularly, not sporadically and not just when you feel like it.

California Governor Jerry Brown, a veteran of over forty years of elected office, continues to take walks with his dog near where he lives. As he walks, people stop him to say hello and to ask questions. Brown always stops and talks. For Brown, the face-to-face contact with "real people" whom he talks to on these walks keeps him grounded and tuned in to real concerns.

"It is real easy to get out of touch when you are an elected official. Most of the people you talk to on a daily basis are insiders who want something. Walking in the neighborhood keeps me in touch with reality," explains Brown.

4. Learn to keep your mouth shut (chapter seven).

During the first few months in office, spend your time learning about your job and the agency you were elected to. Resist the temptation to make big waves. You may have a long list of things that you want to accomplish, but it is going to take time to get them done. Keeping quiet does not mean not asking questions. In your first year, at least, you will want to ask a lot of questions of staff, other elected officials, and the public. At public meetings, guard against feeling compelled to talk to show people how smart you are. We're really not impressed.

Leon Page advises, "I'd encourage newly elected members to pay attention, do their homework, read the agenda packet, ask questions, and always, always be respectful to staff and the public. Modesty in public life is way underrated."

Matt Rexroad, a Yolo County supervisor, agrees: "I would suggest that you encourage newly elected officials to humble themselves. I think they learn more in the first year in office than any other time. Many come in with guns ablaze and then are never able to recover from the problems they have caused."

5. Take advantage of all opportunities to learn.

If your city or agency doesn't have training sessions for elected officials, find out why and demand orientations from the professional staff of the agency. Take advantage of conferences for newly elected representatives. Shirley Concolino, city clerk for the City of Sacramento, observes that relatively few elected leaders take the time to attend training sessions. Those who do, she notes, are always more effective.

New hires, whether they are teachers, parking control officers, or baristas at the local Starbucks, go through training and orientation programs. So should elected officials. Being elected is a significant responsibility, and it is going to take a lot of effort to be good. Regrettably, you will probably have to take your own initiative to find and attend training programs. Most are well worth the effort.

A school board member in Southern California attends training sessions and seminars every chance he gets. He purchases and reads books to learn what others are doing and applies what he has learned to becoming a better board member. "We constantly encourage our students to be life-long learners—why should I be any different?"

6. Surround yourself with people smarter than you and who don't always agree with you.

Local elected officials may not have a lot of staff; most have none. Almost all, however, have a circle of informal advisors and associates who are willing to provide insights and perspectives. Asking for advice is not a sign of weakness. Get different perspectives from people who are not in office. A couple of hours every week should be spent with people (not elected) to look at problems in a new way or from a different perspective.

© 2012 Tom Meyer

Self Reflection

What perks are given to elected officials in your agency? Without needing to adopt an official policy on perks, what is your own policy?

_____

_____

Look at your personal schedule. Make sure that you schedule time to walk precincts, even when there is no election.

_____

_____

Make a point of listening to your colleagues. Find out what issues are important to them.

_____

_____

List the training sessions that are available for elected officials. Make time to attend.

_____

_____

What are the ways you intend to solicit a broad swath of input?

_____

_____

CHAPTER SIX

Getting off on the right foot

© 2012 Tom Meyer

"Sometimes the hardest thing to grasp about leadership is that it is not about you. It's easy to make it about us. We want to do something, so naturally we push, when actually we should be pulling by considering the needs of others first. In leadership, as with so much in life, the more we give, the more we have."

Bob Burg and John David Mann, from their book *It's Not About You*

The period of time between a successful election and taking office is usually very short. Balancing what you want to do and can do (immediately) is always a challenge. Accomplishing your long-term goals will take time. You may have spent many months running for office, but you now have just a few weeks before taking office. Don't wait for your swearing-in to start preparing. Rather than waste time in celebratory events, use your time to get to know key staff and the other elected officials, and become familiar with the issues your elected body will deal with. Pay particular attention to learning about the budget, where money comes from, and how it is spent.

This period is a good time to start developing working relationships with your fellow elected officials (even the ones who may not have been supportive during your campaign). Meet with your new colleagues. Find out what *their* priorities are. What issues do *they* feel are important? Are there things you can work on together? Remember the Rule of Three: If you can't get a majority to agree with you on an issue, you won't get the votes needed to get anything done.

When you were a candidate, staff members, including department heads, were probably willing (perhaps reluctantly) to talk to you. Now that you have been elected, your role and authority have changed. They must talk to you! Use your new position to your advantage. Ask questions. Get reports. Learn as much as you can about the budget, contracts, and pending issues.

Immediately after the election, reach out to your former opponents as well. Don't wait for them to call you. There is no rule that says that you need to wait until your opponents congratulate you. Call them. Congratulate them on their efforts and ask them to sit down and have a conversation. Being gracious in victory is even more important than being gracious in defeat.

The election is over and you represent everyone now. Political battles of the past are far less important than your ability to get things done in the future. Candidates often look at their opponents as the enemy and have a difficult time burying the hatchet. Once the election is over, burying the hatchet is one of the first things that must be done. It serves no one, least of all the public, to have you continue to engage in partisan or personal battles. Take a cue from sports teams (which are as competitive as political campaigns). When the game is over, both sides meet; the combatants shake hands and move on. If there is a postgame press conference, the winning coach or players often acknowledge the great effort of the losing team.

The public does not care about your political battles, and you are expected to work with others to solve problems. Gracefulness in victory is an important part of your own development. Equally important, it is a necessary part of building the relationships that are important to get things done. Remember, one of the greatest challenges of an elected leader is to control the ego. The election is over. Reaching out to your opponents is a smart first step.

When the newly elected mayor of a midsized California city won his election, defeating the incumbent mayor and a current member of the city council, many wondered if the new mayor could govern a divided city. During the vigorously contested election, there were heated disagreements among the candidates. When all the votes were counted it was clear that the new mayor had not been the first choice of most voters (this city had adopted the controversial ranked choice voting system). To complicate things, the new mayor needed the support of the councilwoman he had defeated.

In an act of graciousness that was also smart politically, the mayor-elect agreed to attend a fund-raiser to help pay off the losing candidate's modest campaign debt. While the debt was not large, it was significant that the new mayor attended and symbolically helped the losing candidate and current councilmember. Hatchets were buried, and while the mayor and the councilmember continued to have disagreements on issues, they developed a cordial working relationship.

After presidential elections, the newly elected president has about three months to put together his or her cabinet, pick department heads, and set a legislative agenda. At the local level, many newly elected officials use the time between election and swearing-in to celebrate, rest, and enjoy the perks of their new position (usually in that order). A better strategy is to use that period of time getting to know the people and the problems you are going to be working with.

In your first term in office you will face many issues, some old and some new. You may think you know a lot about your new elected office and the problems you will face, but more often than not, the learning curve is steep. Developing good working relationships with your colleagues and the staff of the agency will be critical if you are to achieve any meaningful progress. Your swearing-in ceremony is a good place to start.

Swearing-in ceremonies differ significantly from one community to another. Some events are formal, others are very casual. Common to all, beyond the oath of office, is that the new representative is the center of attention. People will look to you and listen to what you have to say. Whether you are speaking from the podium or talking informally as you accept congratulations and well wishes, you are the center of attention. The swearing-in ceremony is a great opportunity to get off on the right foot with your new colleagues and the full-time staff of the public entity. Your future success will rest on your relationship with them and their success.

The swearing-in ceremony is also a good time to make the transition from a candidate seeking votes to an elected official representing the entire community, including people who did not support your election.

Celebrate your victory with an abundance of graciousness.

At your swearing in, thank your supporters—but then be gracious to your former opponents and the people who worked against you. If it was a vigorous, competitive election, a good portion of the electorate may have voted against you. Reaching out to your opponents is not a sign of weakness; it is a sign of strength. It's also smart politically, as you may need them at some point to get things done.

Like postgame press conferences, your remarks at your swearing-in speech will be noticed by few and remembered by fewer still. It will be rare for any of it to get any press coverage whatsoever. That is not to say your remarks are not important. They are very important. There are some very important people who are listening carefully and paying close attention.

Here are the people that you are speaking to and who are listening to what you have to say:

- Your new colleagues
- Former and outgoing elected officials
- Critical staff (particularly the city manager, superintendent of schools, department heads, etc., depending on your office)
- Former opponents
- Political insiders
- Your family and close friends

This is a small group of people, but many of them have been or will be critical to your future success. Your swearing-in provides a good opportunity to acknowledge the work of your predecessors but at the same time look toward the future. You can do that in formal remarks or as you speak privately to people. For the most part, the people who attend swearing-in ceremonies are the most insider of the insiders, and they often will interpret to others what you say and what you do. Get off on the right foot. Be humble and gracious. Acknowledge that you have a lot to learn.

Since it is obvious that you will thank those people who have been critical to your success (by name if possible), we won't dwell on that point. Occasionally a newly elected individual, being caught up in the moment, might forget to thank or acknowledge his or her spouse. Don't. But don't go overboard either. Enough said.

There is usually very little press coverage at swearing-in ceremonies at the local level. Why? Because it is not news. The election was newsworthy. What you may do in the future may be newsworthy, but speeches and swearing-in ceremonies are not. Most of the people in attendance are friends and insiders. Why, then, is this opportunity to speak important? There will be many other opportunities in the future.

Your initial swearing-in ceremony is the one opportunity you will have to publicly transition from candidate to elected official. In the few minutes you speak, you will have the opportunity to show people that you are gracious, thoughtful, and up to the task of governance.

In preparing your swearing-in speech, keep in mind the advice of pollster Dr. Frank Luntz. In his book *What Americans Really Want . . . Really*, Dr. Luntz lists ten things Americans want from their elected officials:

1. To be genuine in everything you say
2. To be genuine in everything you do
3. To bring back the gerund—an active verb, the "ing," i.e., doing, working, changing
4. To create and publicize a "getting things done" checklist
5. To ask people what they think, and listen to their answers
6. To acknowledge voters' frustration and empathize with it
7. To individualize, personalize, and humanize your communication with voters
8. To admit a mistake
9. To show a passion for your work and the people you serve
10. To say "Thank You" and show appreciation

Stories are the way we communicate with one another. Throughout history, stories have been the way lessons are passed down from one individual to another and from one generation to another. Develop your storytelling skills. Providing anecdotes to illustrate the importance of a particular action can often provide the "why" of a particular decision. Look for ways you can describe what you want in a manner that people can relate to and in language that people understand.

Funding or replacing sewer lines may seem mundane or unimportant, but the reason for doing so, told through stories, can breathe life into a drab subject. Street repairs may be boring, but explaining why they are needed in ways the average person can understand will help build support. No one wants to pay for more taxes, but describing why a school needs renovations may convince reluctant taxpayers to help foot the bill.

Compelling stories, not drab facts, move people. Develop these skills.

© 2012 Tom Meyer

Self Reflection

Have you reached out to your opponents?

_____

_____

Have you personally thanked all the people that helped you win your election?

_____

_____

Have you made an effort to meet department heads and key staff?

_____

_____

Have you revised your goals based on what you have learned?

_____

_____

Have you personalized your communications?

_____

_____

Are you developing your ability to tell compelling stories?

_____

_____

CHAPTER SEVEN

To lead, start by listening

© 2012 Tom Meyer

"A wise old owl sat on an oak; The more he saw the less he spoke; The less he spoke the more he heard; Why aren't we like that wise old bird?"

Anonymous

You got elected, in part, by talking. Talking at meetings, at debates, at endorsement meetings, on the phone, and at voters' front doors. You made your case for your election in hundreds of conversations. You may have talked about your experience and your bold policy goals, or you may have pointed out the weaknesses of your opponents. People wanted to hear your opinions and your positions on issues, and you were more than happy to give them. Talking must have worked; you won.

Now that you are elected, there is a tendency to think your success in office will again be based on your ability to talk. It won't. As an office holder you need to talk less and work to develop your listening skills. Talking may have gotten you elected, but *listening* will help you be effective in office. Listening will take many forms: listening to colleagues, to staff, to the public, and especially to people who may not have the time to attend a meeting. You will also need to listen to your own instincts.

Unlike a sprinter at a track meet, you do not need to get "off the starting blocks with a bang." You don't even need to make an impact in the first six to twelve months in office. What you need to do is learn everything about your agency and build good working relationships with your colleagues and staff. The relationships you build in the first year are the foundation upon which you will be able to get things done in the months and years that follow.

Keeping your mouth shut and listening requires self-control and discipline. It's not easy. Yet, learning to keep quiet may be one of the most important, albeit most difficult, skills an elected official needs to learn. There is no need to talk to show people how smart and well informed you are on the issues. People expect that elected officials are well informed.

Your first year should be spent listening and observing. If you have to talk, ask questions. Take notes on issues and observe the way other elected officials you respect, or those who are known for getting things done, deal with staff, the public, and other fellow council or board members. The more you listen and ask questions, the easier it will be to differentiate what is important and what is less so, what is doable and what is impractical. By listening when others speak, more people will listen to you when you speak.

Jonathan Daugherty, an elected official in Florida, observes: "There is an old saying, 'It is better to be thought a fool than to open your mouth and prove it.' I had a bad habit of thinking out loud. Initially when I spoke during a meeting I rambled. It got so bad that the mayor had a small hourglass that he would turn over every time I started talking. (This was done in a position that the general public could not see.) To prevent myself from rambling I started writing down a bullet list of my points before the meeting or before I would speak. This allowed me to organize my points before I spoke. I found that by numbering my points and being brief I became much more persuasive. I know from experience when someone is talking for three to four minutes I start to zone out; they may be saying something important but I simply lose attention. I also found myself thinking more about what I was going to say than what my colleague was saying. Once I learned to listen I became much more effective."

Asking questions forces others to articulate their positions. Listening allows you to adjust based on new information or new circumstances.

Fred Ross, Sr., the renowned mentor of Cesar Chavez who trained hundreds of union organizers and scores of community leaders, many of whom eventually became elected leaders, taught two simple rules:

- There is a time for sound and a time for silence, and a good organizer [or elected official] needs to be able to differentiate between the two.
- When you are tempted to make a statement, ask a question.

As a candidate, there were issues that you campaigned on and promises you made that you will not be able to accomplish as immediately or easily as you would like. Say, for example, you campaigned on overhauling the public employee pension system. Accomplishing that may take months, if not years, and it will take delicate, difficult negotiations with the public employee unions. At a minimum, you will also need the support of your other elected colleagues. Your desire to reduce the costs of taxpayer-financed pension plans will not trump the collective bargaining agreements that were negotiated years earlier. The governing process is slow and works against quick or easy decisions. Listening to all sides, weighing the cost and benefits, looking at long-term effects—all are part of effective leadership.

You can't win every issue. You need to prioritize when to go to battle. Not all battles are worth fighting. Determine what battles you want to fight and how long you will need. You may have campaigned on a desire to repair local streets, but limited resources in the budget and other competing city needs may stall your efforts. Your budget at the local level will largely be determined by the economy and politics and policies at the state and national levels, over which you will have no control.

Ken Nordoff, the city manager in Walnut Creek, California, cautions that the bigger the problem, the longer it is going to take to successfully deal with it. The key to tackling *big* issues is to start. Just starting is often the most difficult step. Successfully tackling a tough problem could take tens if not hundreds of meetings and perhaps years. (Remember the old riddle: How do you swallow an elephant? Answer: One bite at a time!)

Most terms of office are four years—1,461 days to make a difference and accomplish your goals. That may seem like a long time, but time moves quickly. Of all of the resources you have, *time* is the most precious and most easily wasted. Getting an early start studying issues, getting to know staff, and developing relationships with your colleagues can help avoid missteps and mistakes along the way.

Voting on legislation is just one small part of the work. The bigger, more difficult part of your job requires leadership. Leadership doesn't automatically happen when someone is elected to office. Leadership is learned and earned over a long period of time by tackling difficult issues and providing guidance and inspiration to others to solve problems.

Eric Zorn, a columnist for the *Chicago Tribune*, writes extensively on local government and politics. On November 3, 2010, his insightful column, *Change of Subject*, provided the newly elected governor of Illinois useful and practical advice, which is relevant for any elected official at any level of government. He also points to the need to listen.

Here are some excerpts from his column with some comments I have added:

First, stay humble . . . don't go thinking you've made the sale with the electorate and have earned a mandate to carry out your agenda, whatever exactly it might be.

Not many people who get elected could be defined as "humble." But the point is a good one. There are many factors that go into being elected, the least of which is that voters agreed with all of your positions. No one is elected with a mandate, no matter how many votes he or she received.

Second, hire people smarter than you are and listen to them. This is not a knock on your intelligence. No one can have his mind fully around all the issues that a governor [elected official] has to deal with, particularly the economic mess, and still run a state.

Dump the "yes" men, the toadies, the lackeys, and the party hacks. Bring into your inner circle at least one person from the other party or with a contrasting political philosophy. Encourage creative dissent in your ranks.

Insist that your advisers and deputies study seriously the policies and reforms instituted in the laboratories of the other states. Sit down with organizational researchers from the left, right, and middle. What works? What doesn't? What's worth trying here?

Unless you ran unopposed, chances are there were many people who didn't vote for you. Solutions to complex problems will require creativity and flexibility. Involving others, even those who disagree with you, to help think through problems will generate practical solutions.

Third, think before speaking. Activists, gadflies, pundits, and lesser elected officials can float ideas, brainstorm aloud, and give into rhetorical impulses, usually with little consequence.

A strong leader doesn't allow controversies to simmer. He/she doesn't announce intentions unless they're backed by solid plans.

There is nothing wrong with floating an idea to get discussions going, but as an elected official your words carry some weight. Think before you talk. Frame your ideas into questions: What would happen if we tried this? Have you given thought to . . .? Could we try this?

Fourth, demonstrate a ferocious commitment to reducing "waste, fraud, mismanagement, and abuse." It's probably not nearly the multibillion-dollar problem in state government that so many critics believe, but the perception that elected officials tolerate it poisons their relationship with the public.

In polling, voters made it clear they want to protect the core services that make up most of the budget, yet don't want to raise any taxes to pay for them, in large part because they don't believe government is making the best use of the tax money it receives. Do you blame them?

So streamline a few agencies. Combine others. Root out redundancies. Put all these moves online and explain them in plain English. That way, when you come forward with your pockets turned inside out pleading poverty, you'll have the credibility to ask for new revenue.

Times change. The rising cost of providing services to the people will require fresh thinking. A hundred years ago, "civil service reform" was the cry of reformers who saw rampant corruption and graft in the old patronage system. Today, the costs associated with providing public employees competitive salaries, benefits, and pensions may require new reforms that protect employees and the public.

Fifth, forget who brought you to the dance. *Yes, a lot of organizations and interest groups poured a lot of money into your campaign, and they expect to be your special pets going forward. But you don't work for them; you work for all of us.*

Voters brought you to the dance, not interest groups. Taxpayer associations, or teachers, or environmental groups may have supported you, but you are elected to represent everyone. Of all the things you should worry about as an elected official, re-election should be the least important.

Sixth, pick your fights wisely and wage most of your battles in private. *There's a fine line between being principled and being stubborn, being a leader and being a grandstander.*

No one wants to see people fight in public unless they are paid to fight. You're not. Your job is to find solutions to problems. As two people in a successful marriage adapt and adjust based on new or unforeseen circumstances, say a new child or a loss of a job, an elected official will have to adapt based on new and changing realities he or she will face in office.

Seventh, think long term. *Though your goal shouldn't be re-election in four years, the truth is it will be a lot easier for you to win [your next election] if you've steadily cut the deficit, whittled at the debt, gradually lowered the unemployment rate, protected core services for the least fortunate, and improved education.*

A tall order, sure, particularly in times like these. But good governing is ultimately good politics, and you and the legislative leaders have to find some way to agree to make tough, even unpopular decisions with an eye not on tomorrow's editorials, but on the scoreboard that will light up several years from now.

No one can predict the future, but we do know that the decisions made today will affect people five, ten, twenty years down the line. Ignoring repairs to infrastructures will add to costs for future generations. Postponing renovations to schools will cost more later. Refusing to streamline services or reduce the size of bureaucracy will create burdens on taxpayers.

Eighth, resolve to be a better communicator. *Put everything you can online. Meet regularly with reporters and with leaders from both parties. At least for now, remember we're all in this together. Good luck.*

Once an election is over, communicating with the public is not the start of anyone's "to do" list. Perhaps it should be. How are you going to incorporate "listening" into your daily routine? If you don't make it a priority now it will not happen.

City Manager Rod Gould would add a ninth item of advice:

Admit your errors.

Admitting errors is really quite unusual in elected life. It will generate respect because it is so rare.

Getting advice from academics, reporters, or even from a book like this and then incorporating that advice into your daily or professional life is difficult. A veteran elected official will have difficulty changing habits and patterns after years in elected office. The newly elected official can develop good habits early on in his or her career. It starts with a plan and a commitment.

Self Reflection

Resolve to be civil at all times. Politics can be personal, but governance is about compromise. Are you willing to compromise?

_____

_____

Think long term. How will your decisions today affect people five, ten, twenty years from now?

_____

_____

Are you controlling the need to talk on every issue?

_____

_____

Do you readily acknowledge your errors?

_____

_____

What steps can you take, right now, to help achieve your goals?

_____

_____

CHAPTER EIGHT

Small steps lead to big wins

© 2012 Tom Meyer

"If you are able to achieve anything big in life it's because you paid attention to the small things."

Fred Ross, Sr., community organizer, trainer of Cesar Chavez

You can't successfully run for office by saying that once elected you are going to slowly make small incremental progress on the big problems, even though that is the reality of being in office. Voters want solutions, and during the campaign most candidates will say they will tackle the big issues: improving public safety, improving education, creating jobs, cutting bureaucracy, reforming pension plans, or getting spending under control. All candidates eventually learn, once they are elected, that there are very few things that happen quickly, or easily. Small steps are the key to long-term progress.

An old adage says that you need to learn to walk before you learn to run. Once you are elected, you need to stop "running" and learn to walk, sometimes slowly. You may have spent a year or more of your life running for office, but once the election is over you need to prepare yourself for the slow, often frustrating pace of governing.

Successful small steps on important issues will eventually add up to big improvements. As a candidate you may have hoped to make Big Changes. You may have promised Big Results, but as an elected official, it is the small decisions that will add up to big changes over time.

David Kersten, a consultant to the California State Assembly, offers this insight: "I believe newly elected officials need to be given more extensive background training in various issue areas. They get in office and want to fulfill a number of their campaign promises but each issue has a long legislative history, so staff ends up researching a bunch of uncooked bill ideas, most of which do not pan out."

Ken Hampian, a retired city manager from San Luis Obispo, who spent more than twenty years orienting and training new council members, makes this observation: "Sincere representatives will realize that things are a lot more complicated than they imagined and that their duties are far, far broader than the issue(s) they campaigned on."

In the course of your term in office, you will look back at just a few situations where you solved *big* issues or made *big* decisions. All significant issues require incremental steps, countless meetings, compromise, small steps, and half steps to make progress.

The big problems you want to fix didn't become big problems overnight, and the problems won't be solved overnight either. Working cooperatively with your elected colleagues (something the public expects at the local level and hardly ever sees at the national level) is necessary to solve problems and make incremental progress.

Most of the decisions you make and the actions you take on a daily basis will fall into the category of small things. But just because they are small does not mean they are insignificant. Taking time to listen to a constituent may result in action that benefits not only that individual, but others who may have similar problems.

As an elected leader, you will find that some of your most important work may fall outside your legislative duties. Some of the most important actions you take will have nothing to do with policy, but rather with getting the public to support a major initiative or even demonstrating concern.

A city council member has a large calendar on his wall, which counts down the days left in his term. Each day he ceremoniously removes one day, saying, "One day less to accomplish our goals. So what are we doing today?" When each day is valued, progress is made.

A newly elected school board member made a point of regularly visiting each school in the district to talk to teachers and principals as well as to custodians and school staff. In the process, her visits boosted morale for employees while she gained keen insights into the challenges each school faced. Over time, as she visited every school, some multiple times, she began to see small, yet important, things that she, as a board member, could accomplish. Things she never would have learned had she not taken the time to visit the schools.

She observed: "I learned that most principals and teachers had never seen a school board member, since none of the other board members ever visit schools. So when I came to visit, they were actually surprised and happy that someone wanted to learn about the schools."

She went on to describe the appalling conditions she found everywhere. "I learned the schools are in poor shape physically. They are run down on the outside and classrooms haven't been renovated in years. I met teachers whose budgets are so tight that they spend their own money for supplies. But I also learned that school supplies were hoarded and not used because principals were worried about funding for the next year. Getting people to talk together didn't seem like much, but in time it made a big difference. I never would have seen or heard things if I had relied on staff to tell me. By being visible I became more knowledgeable."

Her school visits also made her aware of the surrounding neighborhoods—ranging from upper-middle-class areas in the hills, to ethnic and immigrant neighborhoods in the poorer sections of town. She also learned about successes. She learned what was working, and met teachers who were making a difference by recruiting parents to come into the classrooms to volunteer as aides. "Teachers are overwhelmed, unsupported, and unappreciated," she concluded. "They feel so frustrated and alienated. I know I'm only one person, but I know I can make a difference."

As she reported on the conditions of the schools at each school board meeting and in various meetings at each school, she slowly built support for placing a tax measure on the ballot. A facilities improvement task force was created; the business community got involved and eventually the school district passed a bond measure to renovate every school. Her small steps led to a big success.

Some things may seem small to you, but they may be big things to others. Bike lanes, dog parks, zoning rules, and development agreements all are important. Collectively they are what local government is all about. Government can't and probably shouldn't be expected to solve all problems, but the work you do daily can make a big difference in people's lives.

Garrison Keillor wrote in *Time* magazine on August 25, 2003: "Most men and women in politics are there because they genuinely like people and want to do good things on their behalf. It's hard work and fury isn't the best motivation. You have to sit through the meetings, listen to other people, and say your piece and be civil about it . . . [Go] for a walk on a summer night and notice the little ramps carved into curbs at street corners. People sat through a lot of meetings to get that accomplished. It was a boon to the wheelchair crowd and also to parents pushing strollers and kids riding bikes. It made life slightly more civil and friendly. Government works through small, incremental changes . . ."

The key for elected officials, new or seasoned, is to determine what they want to accomplish, set clear priorities, and then work on those issues that are priorities. As a candidate, you had to inspire people to get involved in your campaign. The more people involved, the easier it was to campaign. So too, an elected official needs to inspire and motivate people to work on causes or issues that are important. Continuing to get people involved after you are elected will make it a lot easier to accomplish what you want.

Successful candidates often talk about keeping their campaign volunteers active and involved once a campaign is over, but they rarely do. It is too bad, because volunteers, working in cooperation with elected officials, can tackle problems that may be too small for a legislative fix or outside the responsibilities of government.

A candidate we worked with, who successfully ran for the board of supervisors, was concerned about the increased rates of smoking among young people. When a discount tobacco store announced it was opening a retail outlet in her district near a high school, she mobilized her volunteers. Together they collected signatures opposing the business; they spoke to high school classes about the dangers of smoking and its link to cancer and other health problems. A problem became an opportunity to educate and organize. Eventually the store decided not to open. All of this was due to campaign volunteers keeping active and involved.

In another community former campaign volunteers worked to convince a grocery chain that had many communities vying for it to open a store in an underserved area. The store admitted that one of the factors in choosing the new location was the community support.

You don't have to tackle the biggest issue or the toughest issue. In *On Being a Teacher*, Jonathan Kozol says, "Pick battles big enough to matter, small enough to win." Successful organizers know that small victories, small successes lead to bigger victories and bigger successes. Equally important, successes (even small ones) can boost spirits and morale to keep people engaged and inspired.

Tackling difficult or controversial problems can seem daunting. Leadership sometimes requires taking unpopular positions. The best decisions are rarely the most popular. Cutting budgets, consolidating services, supporting new construction, or campaigning for tax increases often requires difficult decisions that may upset some people.

Regardless of the office held, elected officials are in a great position to lead and to get people involved. That is part of the power of office. Use your position and authority to get the things done that need to get done. Organizing shouldn't stop when you get elected. Ask people to come to meetings and to work on issues that are important. Recruit volunteers to work on projects. The more people involved the better.

© 2012 Tom Meyer

Self Reflection

Review your larger goals. What are the small steps that could help achieve your goals?

_____

_____

How do you maintain momentum on a particular initiative?

_____

_____

What problems could volunteers work on?

_____

_____

Are you working to involve citizens in solving problems? How?

_____

_____

How do you monitor your progress?

_____

_____

CHAPTER NINE

Working with the chief executive

© 2012 Tom Meyer

"Coming together is a beginning; keeping together is progress; working together is success."

Henry Ford

Almost seven hundred years ago in Siena, Italy, Ambrogio Lorenzetti created a fresco in the Palazzo Pubblico (town hall). The fresco illustrates good government and bad government and the effect each would have on the city and the country. The frescoed walls decorating the council room of the Siena City Hall consist of six different scenes: *Allegory of Good Government*, *Allegory of Bad Government*, *Effects of Bad Government in the City*, *Effects of Good Government in the City*, *Effects of Good Government in the Country*, and *Effects of Bad Government on the Country*.

These fading frescoes depict in graphic detail what happens when there is good government and when there is not. In the fresco illustrating the effect of good government, we see prosperity, abundant harvests, work, music, peace, and celebrations. Conversely, the fresco illustrating bad government portrays crime, poverty, corruption, pestilence, and disease. The message in these frescos is that good government doesn't happen by chance or luck. It takes hard work, cooperation, and the efforts of many. This concept is as relevant today as it was seven hundred years ago.

Many of the decisions or actions you take as an elected official are small, but there are a few big decisions that you will make that you need to get right. During your term in office you may have the opportunity (assuming you have the support of others on your board) to select the chief executive of your agency. Your selection may well determine whether you have a good government, a bad one, or merely an ineffective one.

Nothing is more important or more critical to get right than the selection of the chief executive. No city council or mayor is successful without a competent chief administrator or city manager. No school district or school board member will be successful without a quality superintendent of schools.

The person *you* select for these positions will determine *your* success. A poor selection will drain the district's (taxpayers') resources, lead to significant personnel disruption, and may negatively affect the community for years. Your own reputation, good or bad, will be tied to the successes or failures of the chief executive. When you have the opportunity to select a new chief executive, you need to make a great choice.

Earlier we gave credit to former Oakland Mayor Jerry Brown (now California Governor Brown) for his ability to follow through on his vision to bring new housing to downtown Oakland. Much of Mayor Brown's success should be credited to the skill and leadership of the competent city manager of Oakland at that time, Robert Bobb. Mr. Bobb, in turn, hired competent department heads who, along with Mr. Bobb, were able to move the city bureaucracy in a direction that fulfilled Mayor Brown's vision.

Mr. Bobb made sure that every department head and every employee knew what the mayor's vision was, and he made it clear to either get on board or go somewhere else. A bit dramatic perhaps, but effective. Without the experience and the skills of Mr. Bobb, it is unlikely that Mayor Brown would have achieved the level of success he desired. While Mayor Brown and Mr. Bobb often had disagreements, they shared a common vision and common purpose.

City Manager Rod Gould observes that the relationship between the top executive and the elected board is critically important and must allow for give and take to provide honest feedback to the top executive and back to the board members. This is critical if the agency is to run well. "While there are formal (usually annual) performance reviews, these reviews can be awkward, and both sides often avoid them. But everyone loses when poor decisions are made. Managers, superintendents, general managers, councils, boards, and the public are best served with clear goals and expectations and regular discussions of how the executives are managing."

Replacing or hiring a new chief executive is time consuming, difficult, and expensive. Finding the right executive is not easy, despite the efforts and hefty fees of individuals who do executive searches. Be aware that you can be the victim of being passed a lemon. It may be years before you know if the person you hired had the "right stuff." That being said, a new leader may require a period of time to find his or her "sea legs." Be sure to provide clear expectations regarding what you want and need in order for this new leader to be effective. Conducting annual evaluations is an effective way of doing this.

Kids often play a game called hot potato. The potato is passed from one person to another. The object of the game is to make sure you don't get stuck with the potato. If the game ends and you are holding the potato, you lose. Elected officials often play a similar game, with even more serious results. They call it passing the lemons. Here is how it is played.

An elected board of a city, a school district, or other governmental agency has a chief executive it wants to replace. Rather than going through the difficult process of evaluating, and perhaps firing, this person, the elected leaders make sure the person they want to replace has good recommendations so when he or she is considered for another job the position will be offered to the person. When interviews are conducted, board members make sure to say something positive, lest the person not get the job. This is called passing the lemons—having your problems become somebody else's.

Hiring is expensive, and bad personnel decisions can be costly. It's important to do plenty of research before entrusting your city, school district, or agency to someone you are not fully and completely sure has the skills, temperament, and motivation to do an outstanding job. Make sure you are not trying to make lemonade out of someone else's discarded lemons. Research suggests that personal references are a better predictor of an employees' success than his/her performance at an interview.

When she hires key staff, Shirley Concolino, city clerk for Sacramento, California, never completely relies on resumes, references, or recommendations from recruitment consultants. Clerk Concolino knows that resumes are often padded, and no sane person applying for a job would list as a reference someone who wasn't supportive. To find out as much as she can before hiring someone, Ms. Concolino personally calls people who have previously worked with the prospective employee. Ms. Concolino knows that a poor hire can cause disruption and a waste of resources and time.

Selecting the right chief executive takes research and a disciplined, focused board. The right choice will bring new energy and new ideas. The wrong choice can bring disaster. How do you start? While executive search companies and job postings will identify potential candidates, you need to do your own independent research. Start with the Internet. Ample information is available on the qualities to look for in a new chief executive, as well as specific information on an individual you may be considering. Remember, this hire is the most important hire you will make in your term of office. Rely on experts and consultants to help, but rely on your own instincts and your own research as well.

What track record does the person have? Success breeds success. Rarely is a person successful in one place after being unsuccessful in an earlier situation. A strong personality, good communication skills, and an impressive resume are all reasonable qualifications, but they are not enough.

As a board, you will need to clearly articulate your goals and what this new leader will be expected to do. Your chief responsibility, as a board member, is to make sure the entire board is in agreement as to the expectations and goals. Make sure whomever you hire has a clear understanding of what your board expects. Hoping the person will succeed is not enough. Regularly evaluating the person, once hired, will be a lot easier if clear expectations are established up front and agreed upon.

One of the idiosyncrasies of local government is that the chief executive is hired by and reports to the board, but he or she will also be expected to mentor the board. You will hire the person, but then need to rely on this person to lead. City Manager Ken Hampian says: "The chief executive's role is to lead the organization in a positive, productive, and highly ethical way so that council members feel adequately supported and do not need to invest time in resolving organizational conflicts, performance deficiencies, or ethical breaches." Does your chief executive exhibit these qualities?

The role of the chief executive of a public agency is similar to the role of a team coach. The success of the team will be based on the ability of the team members to work well together. The coach's job is to make sure the players fit the right roles. A successful superintendent or city manager will size up the talents of the board members and make sure they are assigned to committees based on their abilities and interests. The willingness of the elected board to work in collaboration with the chief executive is critical for the success of the agency.

The public expects elected officials to get things done. What the public doesn't readily recognize is that despite the best efforts of elected officials, the permanent bureaucracy can impede or delay progress. The chief executive is the one person who can make the bureaucracy move. He or she is the one who can pick up a good idea from the council or the public and turn that idea into action. Implementing change is usually complex, and it takes leadership and patience to make it happen. It won't happen without a good chief executive.

Kathleen Millian, city manager of Santa Rosa, California, acknowledges that even in the best of circumstances where council members work well together, it takes the leadership of the "hired staff" to convert ideas into action.

She observes, "*The process is oftentimes equally as important as the final decision.* Our method of governance relies on civility and legal due process, and so decision making is often incremental and time consuming, especially on complex issues. This is usually frustrating to everyone. Some newer and some older elected officials want government to run more like private business. Certain processes can be run in this manner, but cutting corners and limiting due process and often transparency leads to trouble with a capital *T*. Even if the decision is a good one and makes good business sense, if the process is poorly run or absent, the final decision will be contested and not credible. So much time, good ideas, and effort are lost because of this."

"Great ideas filter through to council and staff all the time. Determining what's possible, what's legal, what will make things better, and then how to get it done is usually complex. Government staff can be innovative doers; they just have to think through the regulatory responsibility to be able to answer the 'how to do it' question. And, don't forget about your colleagues. Everything takes money and staff time (which is money). Make sure that communication of the idea is done properly with the entire council before actions get under way. Everybody should be able to share in the public kudos received for being effective and responsive; it's empowering to the entire group, elected and staff included."

© 2012 Tom Meyer

Self Reflection

What are the skills and attributes you would want in a chief executive?

_____

_____

What is the process you would use to ensure the effective hiring of a CEO?

_____

_____

How will you avoid getting passed a lemon?

_____

_____

Whose opinion do you trust in identifying potential candidates? Are you willing to personally call references?

_____

_____

How will your board communicate their expectations of the CEO?

_____

_____

CHAPTER TEN

Working with staff

© 2012 Tom Meyer

"I suppose leadership at one time meant muscles; but today it means getting along with people."

Mohandas K. Gandhi

While you have been elected to serve on a board, like it or not, you also have been elected to be part of a bureaucracy, and in many instances, a *big* bureaucracy. City and county governments, school districts, transportation agencies, hospital districts, and other public agencies have lots of employees. In many communities the public agency is the largest employer.

Your ability to get things done will be based on the competence of the people who manage this large governmental bureaucracy. It is the paid staff of this bureaucracy who provide information to you so you can make budget and policy decisions. They will also implement policies and programs the elected board approves. So the "we" now includes the hired staff of the agency you are elected to lead.

No single factor is more important to a well-running public agency than competent staff. But unless you are an elected mayor in a "strong mayor" city, staff does not report directly to you. Staff reports to the city manager, the superintendent, or the general manager of the district, not you. *You* are not *their* boss. You can't micromanage them and you can't go around the chain of command and involve yourself in personnel matters or day-to-day activities to get something you want, no matter how tempting or worthwhile.

Your focus needs to be on big-picture issues. You are helping to steer a big ship. Staff may keep the ship moving, but you determine the direction the ship is going. Getting the ship to the proper destination is your job.

The job of the professional staff is to run the agency and deliver services to the public. Your job is to set policy and budget decisions. While you don't direct staff, your relationship with them is critically important. *You* cannot be effective if you work poorly with staff or if you try to circumvent them.

Despite public opinion bemoaning public employees, most public employees are diligent and want to do a good job. Many have been selected in a highly competitive process that rewards merit, qualifications, experience, and effectiveness. Some hold technical degrees (engineering, urban planning, etc.) and have valuable experience and knowledge in their respective fields. In most cases, they have been there longer than you and will be there long after you leave office.

The relationship between the elected official and the paid staff of the governmental agency is, at best, sensitive. Elected officials must demand quality and competence. At the same time, you do not lead the agency; your role is to set policy.

Establishing a good working relationship is critical to get quality analysis, buy-in, and support. Hardworking employees who are striving for improvement need to be supported and appreciated.

Of course there are ineffective employees, but most public employees take pride in their work. Staff in a public agency provide a critical role. Good staff need to be nurtured, and inspired by vision and goals for the future. But the specifics of implementation need to be left up to them. Your job is to create high expectations and to demand high-quality performance to make sure staff are working in the best interests of the public.

Despite tenure, experience, or even ability, staff are not infallible and need to be held accountable. At times, they may not be providing you with all the answers or all the options. Working often outside the public eye, the elected office holder is dependent on the performance of these employees. Former Menlo Park City Council Member Micki Winkler says: "Coming into office, I was totally dependent on staff for all information. I barely had time to absorb all the new material, much less question it. Yet skepticism is required."

Developing a balance between being supportive and being skeptical is critical. Former Red Bluff City Manager Martin Nichols says, "While elected representatives approve 95 percent of the recommendations that staff make to them, when they do question recommendations or vote *no* on issues is when the system really works well."

Elected officials represent the public and need to always question the bureaucracy. Are we getting the best for what we spend? Can we do things better? Will a new proposal help or hurt the public? Have staff looked at other options? Would staff ever make a recommendation that would eliminate their jobs? As an elected official you must make sure the bureaucracy serves the public and not the bureaucracy itself.

Rod Gould adds that today an effective council member must understand that in an era of shrinking tax revenues and additional cost of providing services, it may not be possible to add new services or programs. He cautions, "Don't simply add additional goals, objectives, and service demands on an already beleaguered staff that is being reduced through attrition or layoff, with furloughs for those who remain. The elected officials need to be clear with each other, the community, and staff about what won't be done given the reduced level of resources and shrunken staff that characterize most public agencies today. At some point, you can't do more with less, but instead decide what to do less of."

One of the challenges of elected officials, if they have been elected in a jurisdiction that has districts, is to balance district needs with the needs of the overall community. This can often cause conflict and disagreement on the allocation of resources. There is no easy solution to this problem, but elected officials, once they are elected, need to understand that they are elected to serve the entire community, not merely the people in the geographical area that they represent.

The professional staff can help in that process, as they serve the entire city or county jurisdiction as well. When they analyze a particular issue or make specific recommendations, they will need to take into account several things: data, institutional needs, history, impacts on the public, law, and cost. They should not take into account the political agenda, relationships, or politics of any one elected leader. This can be difficult at times.

An effective superintendent of schools in a large urban school district almost lost his job because he recommended closing a school in the district of a powerful board member. Rather than looking at the needs of the entire district, the board member, who faced re-election, fought to keep the school open, although keeping the school open was not in the best interest of the entire school district.

City Manager Ken Hampian has worked with hundreds of elected officials during his career. He shares his top ten attributes of a good elected official.

1. Humble enough to have "aha" moments. Quickly sees that governing is more complicated than it looks from the outside (as is the organization); actively seeks to learn and grow during tenure.

Humility is an ongoing theme. Most people we talked to say humility can be learned. It starts with attitude: "I don't know everything." "I can learn from others." "I will learn from my mistakes."

2. *Respects the professionals' role and staff's duty.* *Understands that staff can help manage their difficult work; accepts, however, that staff must play an objective role and follow certain protocols to protect the system long-term.*

Staff will usually be around a lot longer than the average elected official. They have seen many come and go. Part of the staff's job is to act independently and without regard to the wishes of an individual elected official.

3. *Behaves with civility toward staff, toward one another.* *Knows that they collectively represent the community and how they act matters; works to set the right example; does not exploit the staff or colleagues for selfish reasons.*

Rod Gould cautions that it is extremely important to avoid bashing staff: "If you are unhappy with performance or attitude, take it up with the chief appointed officer behind closed doors. Staff bashing will lead to angry, discouraged, and risk-averse administration."

4. *Works as a team—even when there is disagreement.* *Knows that individual success is intertwined with the group's ability to function as an effective, respectable governing body; sees elected colleagues as a vital constituency needed to get things done; avoids grandstanding at expense of others.*

Not everyone on a team gets to score. Not everyone gets to talk to the press after a win. Part of being elected is to find a way to get others to agree with you. The elected representative who goes to the press first or around his or her elected colleagues will have a hard time being successful.

5. Plays fair, honestly. *Works through the manager and department heads; doesn't angle with the staff for special information or treatment; does not stake out absolute positions before public hearings; isn't a sand-bagger.*

I've heard many an elected official say, "Oh, I already know how I am going to vote. We are just having the public hearing because we are required to." Public discussion can be tedious, but it is necessary and required because the public has to have a voice. Access to special information or moving things forward without input from others may work in private industry, but it rarely works in public.

6. Does their homework. *Reads staff reports and asks questions before meetings (to extent possible); tours sites; sincerely listens to reports and testimony; attends workshops and conferences to develop added skills and knowledge.*

Being in office is a lot of work. No one forced you to do it. If you are unwilling to put in the time, let someone else do it.

7. Makes decisions and provides clear direction. *After all reasonable information has been considered, is able to act; doesn't* *procrastinate by asking for endless studies or more information. Decisions and priorities are clearly expressed.*

The easiest way to avoid making decisions is to ask for another report or to appoint another committee to study things. Later on in the book we discuss the "culture of can't." Bureaucracies naturally resist change and new ideas. Your job is to push.

8. Knows when to push—and when to protect. *Able to push staff outside of comfort zone—with discretion; also considers reasonable cautions, fiscal and workload impacts. Protects the staff from abuse; tolerant of occasional human errors (doesn't drive mistakes underground with excessive public "lashings").*

At most council or board meetings there is an agenda item for acknowledging the good work (usually at retirement) of various staff members. While nice, this is not enough. Send notes to people who have done a good job. Take time to acknowledge the work that people do that allows you to take the credit.

9. Provides adequate resources. *Recognizes that there are limits to "doing more with less"—and if a lot more is desired (e.g., a new program, service level) knows that the goal must be properly resourced in order to be accomplished.*

Making a list of priorities is easy. Eliminating or reducing funding for non-priorities is difficult. Sometimes you have to do what's unpopular and explain why you are making the decision. If there isn't proper funding to do a project it won't get done.

10. Knows when to say "no"—and doesn't feed the beast! *Resists trying to be all things to all people; recognizes that overly investing in naysayers will only breed more naysayers.*

The critics of government are loud and vociferous. Engaging the Tea Party activists or the Occupy Wall Street protestors tit for tat will rarely accomplish anything. The naysayers and the critics can occupy all your time if you let them.

The challenge for any elected official is to put these best practices to work. Like a person who wants to lose weight, it doesn't happen easily. Although it may seem simple (drink lots of water, write down everything you eat, eat smaller portions, exercise moderately daily, etc.), it doesn't happen easily or overnight. Lapses are common, predictable, and normal.

Here are some helpful tips to stay on track.

- Listen intently.
- Acknowledge you are not an expert. Be inquisitive.
- Prepare ahead of time.
- Don't play to the crowd or to the moment. Think long term.
- Develop an annual process to set goals, review plans, and measure progress.
- Strive to improve.

One final note that has been mentioned by many: Take time to celebrate the success and accomplishments of the staff. While expensive parties and retreats are not necessary, taking the time to acknowledge superior effort and quality work is always a good use of time. The elected official may be the person who the public sees and who gets the credit when things go well, but usually it is the staff, working behind the scenes, who has contributed to the success. It's important to showcase the benefits of teamwork.

© 2012 Tom Meyer

Self Reflection

How would you grade your relationship with key staff members?

_____

_____

How could you improve your relationship with each? Be specific.

_____

_____

How do you celebrate the successes of employees?

_____

_____

What process do you have in place to support the meaningful review of existing programs and positions?

_____

_____

Are you mindful of the way in which you question and request information from staff?

_____

_____

CHAPTER ELEVEN

Making meetings effective

© 2012 Tom Meyer

"I do not go to a meeting merely to give my own ideas.
If that were all, I might write my fellow members a letter.
But neither do I go simply to learn other people's ideas. If
that were all, I might ask each to write me a letter. I go to a
meeting in order that all together we may create a group idea,
an idea which will be better than all of our ideas
added together."

Mary Parker Follett, social worker, management consultant

A significant part of the work of elected officials takes place in meetings: council meetings, board meetings, commission meetings, special meetings, briefing meetings, community meetings, and staff meetings. There are pre-meeting meetings, postmortem meetings, and personnel meetings. The list goes on and on.

Not only will you be spending a lot of time in meetings, but you will be expected to come to these meetings prepared. That means reading reams of material that needs to be assimilated and understood prior to the meeting. For every hour you spend in meetings, two hours of preparation may be required.

It is impossible to eliminate all meetings (many are legally required), but keeping the meetings focused and on point will save countless hours of your time and staff time.

Some of the best ideas on making meetings more effective come from the experience of elected officials. Here are some of their suggestions:

- Either the mayor or the president of the board or council should develop or control the agenda and meeting. If the president runs a tight ship the meeting will run smoothly; if not, meetings can go on and on.

- Don't ramble. Make notes of what you want to say and stay on point.
- If you don't have something really important to say, don't say anything. It is okay not to speak. It is also preferable, not just for the sake of shorter meetings, not to speak on every issue. Speak only when you have something important to say.
- When you speak or give a report, remember that no one cares to hear that you visited the Happy Trails Children's Center or that you spoke to the Cub Scouts or the local Rotarians during the week.
- Follow the rules regarding public comments. Don't make exceptions. Nothing disrupts the normal flow of meetings more than continual abuse of the public comment portion of public meetings. A two-minute time limit on public comment is a two-minute time limit.
- Do not be intimidated by crowds or disruptive people. Special interests of all stripes and ideologies have learned how to pack meetings and disrupt proceedings to try to get their way. Remember, no matter how many people pack a room, your job is to represent all the people, not just those who come to city hall or the board room or council chambers.
- Come prepared. Much of what is presented at board meetings has already been provided to you in your board packet. Read it ahead of time. Do your homework. Use the meetings to clarify and discuss.

- Provide clear direction to staff. Make sure reports are provided to you ahead of time and that the staff provides summaries or highlights of the most important points. Don't hesitate to ask questions and gather necessary information prior to the meeting.
- Be prompt. If a meeting is scheduled to start at 7:00, start at 7:00, not 7:30 or 7:45.
- Set an example and try to get your fellow elected representatives to agree to common rules. Some of your colleagues may think that they need to comment on everything. They don't.
- Become an expert at managing your meetings. Attend a training session about managing public meetings.
- In developing agendas for meetings, don't load up topics that will take you past midnight. Special meetings covering just one issue may be necessary for really tough topics that will consume an entire evening.

Ironically, televised meetings have added to the length of meetings as everyone, including elected officials, want their two minutes of fame. Years ago, before meetings were televised, recorded, and "YouTubed," it may have been easier for an elected official to speak candidly or even to think out loud. Today, it is the rare meeting that is not recorded in one manner or another, so it is necessary to think before talking. A misstatement or an angry outburst recorded on a smart phone can be downloaded and sent to thousands of people who never attended the original meeting.

John Nalbandian, of the University of Kansas, reminds local elected officials to remember that they are not in Congress or the state legislature. "Saying things on television or in public that are transparently political or self-interested diminishes your respect among your colleagues," he cautions. He urges elected officials to control their urge to speak on all issues. He says that for the sake of effective meetings (and relationships with colleagues), every council member does not have to speak on every issue. Your two cents may not be worth two cents. You are often better off listening than talking.

A well-respected doctor was elected to serve on a five-member governing board of a hospital district. The governing board sets broad policy for the hospital, yet the doctor took every opportunity at every meeting to lecture his colleagues on the nuances of medicine, equipment, and the relationships between doctors, nurses, and staff. While his knowledge was appreciated, his constant lecturing to his colleagues and the public soon wore thin, as did his effectiveness as a member of the board. Finding individuals who were willing to serve with this loquacious, domineering, and opinionated doctor became a problem. Only through intervention was the doctor persuaded that his behavior at meetings was harming the governance of the hospital.

The effective public official, like the effective business leader, learns a lot by asking questions of the people doing the work. The day-to-day managers and the people providing services to the public often have good ideas, but are rarely listened to. What ideas do they have to make things more efficient? What ideas do individual teachers have to improve their schools? Asking questions often leads to new insights and new perspectives.

Parking control officers in one city suggested that giving people a five-minute grace period before writing a ticket could calm angry people and lessen disputes between the public and parking control officers who enforce parking rules. The city implemented this policy on a temporary basis. Complaints went down and city revenues from parking fines remained constant.

In earlier times, it was easy to learn what people thought by going to the local general store or to a town hall meeting. While we have more tools to communicate than ever before, elected officials today may be more isolated than ever.

Infinite amounts of information are now available to anyone through the Internet. Yet many of us have articles automatically sent to us on topics that we are already interested in. Few of us, elected or not, search out information or opinions we disagree with. We generally search out information to add strength to our positions, rather than search for information that challenges us. Worse still, we tend to talk to people we agree with and who share our perspectives.

Elected officials can easily become isolated and overly influenced by people who have a personal stake in a decision. Interest groups and insiders can dominate discussions as well as public comment at public meetings. A community organization dependent on funding may lobby council members. Parents may oppose the closing of a school despite declining enrollment. Decisions should not be made that pander to one group or another. An effective leader must strive to listen to many voices, not the loudest.

Leon Page offers this perspective: "I'd encourage newly elected members to pay attention, do their homework, read the agenda packet, ask questions, and always, always be respectful to staff and the public."

Audrey Herbrich, a local elected official in Texas, adds that if you listen with sincerity and care, you have a communications advantage. People want to feel that their views are listened to and respected, even though you may disagree.

To get reliable and balanced information, it is necessary to go outside of your circle of friends and acquaintances and the insiders in a community. You need to seek out other opinions. Communicate to the public when they are *not* expecting it. You will be surprised by how many people respond.

Questionnaires and surveys can be a great way to "listen." People like to be asked their opinions on issues; questionnaires and surveys can be a rich source of gathering information about the issues that concern them. Questionnaires can be sent in the mail or distributed door to door or taken online. The results from these questionnaires often provide keen insights that otherwise would not have been shared.

The need to communicate with citizens is more important today than ever before. Public agencies are dependent on voter support to improve facilities, approve budgets, and provide additional revenue for programs. Public schools now compete for dollars in a very competitive arena, since they are up against private schools and charter schools in vying for students, support, and money. Transit agencies and library systems all need public support and tax dollars to improve services and programs.

Regrettably, many public agencies don't listen to the public at all. They are often sensitive and overly cautious about spending money to communicate to the public. Aggressively trying to find out what the public feels about issues, whether they are tax issues, efforts to deal with crime, new regulations regarding parking, or countless other matters, would save public agencies thousands of dollars in the long run. It is not easy. Public forums and public notices are limited at best. To really listen, an agency needs to go out of its comfort zone; questionnaires, surveys, and direct communication tools are essential.

Rod Gould provides this important perspective: "Civic engagement is an increasingly important aspect of governing. A public hearing is perhaps the worst possible way to expect residents to engage with their local governments. Encourage staff to come up with alternative means to get other than the usual suspects involved in the process. This does not apply to mundane decisions such as whether or not to replace the front-end loader, but instead to those decisions that are likely to cause significant change and concern amongst the populous. Neighborhood meetings with small group breakouts, charettes, open houses, surveys, information booths, and coffee klatches can be excellent ways to involve people in community decision making. This breeds better decisions and more support for the government in doing so. This field is evolving, and elected officials should pay attention to it."

© 2012 Tom Meyer

Self Reflection

If your meetings are televised, observe yourself. Did you need to speak? If you did, did you speak clearly and succinctly?

_____

_____

Are you speaking one-fifth of the time if there are five individuals in the meeting? Ask a good friend (who will be honest with you) if you ramble or talk too much.

_____

_____

Schedule a walkabout and talk to employees. Ask questions. Get opinions on issues that you are facing. What questions will you ask?

_____

_____

What are new ways you can gather relevant information?

_____

_____

Make sure you are seeking out opinions and perspectives of people who may disagree with you. Whom can you speak with who holds opinions that differ from yours?

_____

_____

CHAPTER TWELVE

Taking risks is required to make progress

© 2012 Tom Meyer

The difference between a successful person and a failure is not [that] one has better abilities or ideas, but the courage that one has . . . to take calculated risk—and to act."

Andre Malraux (1903–1976),
novelist and former French Minister of Cultural Affairs

The newly elected official will very quickly discover that improving the quality or efficiency of government, be it modest or more significant, is not easy. While there are many challenges, one of the biggest is overcoming the inertia of government itself. Government works slowly, in part, due to the checks and balances that are in place to limit one branch of government or one group of people from gaining too much power. Checks and balances are part of our democratic system, but they slow things down. Getting buy-in, compromising, public meetings, study sessions, and waiting for staff reports also take time.

But even disregarding the institutional checks and balances and the natural sluggishness of governance, government also works slowly because many of the people who are drawn to public employment (and we include public school employees here as well) are not risk takers. Many people desire work in governmental agencies because they offer safe, predictable employment, predictable salaries with predictable raises, predictable vacation schedules, and (usually generous) predictable pensions.

People who work in governmental bureaucracies rarely want to rock the boat or take significant risks. Public employee contracts and civil service rules can also impede progress and change. Doing something different or new is generally not rewarded, and so change does not happen quickly or easily. It is a lot easier and less risky to study problems or ignore problems than to solve them.

In business it is a common truism that one cannot be successful without assuming some risk. Risk entails an element of uncertainty. In government, doing things in a new or innovative way creates challenges for the bureaucracy and the people that work in the bureaucracy. Making changes, doing something new, or questioning how things have been done in the past are sure to meet resistance.

Elected leaders, at some point in their careers, if they want to make a difference, will need to get the bureaucracy to do things in a different way and to try new things. It may be necessary to upset the status quo. Every decision an elected official makes will entail some risk—the risk of failure, the risk of upsetting people, and the risk of doing nothing. Assessing the degree of risk to make progress and then taking appropriate action is part of being a leader.

When you made the decision to run for office you demonstrated that you were willing to take risks. Most likely, you took a financial risk, and perhaps a professional one, to run for office. Your willingness to be judged publicly (and maybe rejected) by voters and to be criticized publicly by your opponents or in the press is a risk that many people are unwilling to take. You did this ostensibly because you wanted the government agency to run better. You were willing to take risks, not for the thrill, but because you wanted to make positive improvements for your community.

What are some of the risks you may have to deal with in office? What are the costs and benefits of each risk? One risk may be trying to do things in a new way. For instance, public employee unions have been able to limit what volunteers can do to clean up public spaces.

This may make sense to the unions who want to protect the jobs of their members, but it may not make sense to the public who would like to volunteer to clean up a park, a creek bed, a school ground, or a median strip in their neighborhood. Finding compromise and agreement to work through a challenge like this will take leadership and a willingness to assume some risk.

In many communities, it is becoming more common to see ballot measures asking voters to repeal binding arbitration rules or modify pensions for police and firefighters. This is a controversial and difficult process and poses risks for the elected officials who consider or support such an option. Firefighters and police officers are not likely to give up or modify benefits without a battle. The elected officials proposing modifying contracts will risk being opposed in their re-election campaigns.

Closing schools and spending money to modernize schools are risks for school board members. Placing a tax measure on the ballot that will increase taxes is another risk. But doing so may be the only way to keep libraries open, keep schools repaired, or maintain existing levels of public service that the public desires. There is the risk of criticism and the obvious risk that voters will reject the proposal. Reducing services because they are too expensive or they are not needed and negotiating new labor agreements are examples of risks for city council members.

Most, if not all, significant decisions will have proponents and opponents. Every decision has the potential of upsetting someone. Every elected official who supports a tax increase, no matter how critical or necessary, will face criticism from opponents. Even the most benign proposal to do something new will have proponents and opponents.

Accomplishing any significant goals will entail risk. In assessing risk, you need to first look at your own reasons for wanting to be elected. Whatever your reasons, you made a pledge when you were sworn in to act in the best interest of the entire community. You didn't take a pledge to take the easiest or the safest route.

Ken Farfsing, a city manager from Southern California, tells this story:

"People are not so much afraid of risks; they are afraid of failing. Our council took a risk, at my urging, and placed a utility tax on the ballot to fund the construction of a new police station. It failed miserably—only a 42 percent approval rate! However, the lesson is not so much about taking risks, it is about what you do to recover after you fail. It took us five years of additional work, but we found another way to construct the new police station. It opens up this year. Had we not taken the risk and lost, we still would not have our new police station."

I have been asked many times by school leaders if I could *guarantee* success if they placed a tax measure on the ballot. As much as I would like to provide a guarantee, and even assuming the measure is put on the ballot with proper care and study, there are no risk-free decisions. No one wants to pay more taxes, but taxes pay for the things that people want.

With city revenues down, city leaders in the City of Santa Monica hoped that voters would pass a small sales tax increase to maintain the existing level of services (libraries, police, fire, etc.). Without this small tax increase, the city would have had no choice but to cut services. The local school district, not part of city government, also needed money and had recently failed to get voter approval for its own parcel tax. I encouraged Rod Gould, the city manager of Santa

Monica, and Tim Cuneo, the superintendent of the school district, to get together to explore how they could help each other.

We crafted a new and creative way to share resources and worked together to pass a tax measure that helped both the city and the schools. It took fresh thinking and a willingness to work together to make it happen. Initially, the plan was seen as risky because no one had tried it before and there was not legal precedent.

To minimize the risk, city leaders in Santa Monica, through the leadership of City Manager Gould, reached out to the public in meetings and newsletters. City leaders met with business leaders and potential opponents to explain the process and the reasons the measure was needed. The school district, through its own leadership and volunteers, reached out to parents, teachers, and the community.

Leaders from both agencies assessed the risk of not acting and decided to move forward. Support was not universal and there were vocal critics. But once the measure was placed on the ballot, the public voted overwhelmingly in favor of the measure. In the end, the perceived risk turned out to be greater than the actual risk.

Since then, other cities have tried to follow Santa Monica's example, and not all have been successful. Each community is different. Tax increases may not be successful the first time you try, but if it is important and you persevere, you may succeed.

Balancing your desire to make progress while protecting the public's assets can be a challenge. You are the caretaker of the public's money and responsible for the effective running of the public agency you were elected to serve. Even in the best economic times, tough decisions will need to be made. You will have to prioritize the best uses of public money.

The easiest thing to do, however, is to do nothing. Risk-averse public agencies often follow this path. As policy makers you and your colleagues will need to assess the benefits of taking risks with the cost of doing nothing.

In business, lawyers are often asked to help assess the risk of doing one thing or another and to help business leaders weigh legal and financial risks against potential reward and then make decisions accordingly. Business leaders know that without risk there is no gain.

Most government agencies either have a department or an individual responsible for risk management. However, these offices, more often than not, operate with a "culture of can't." (We can't do this; we can't do that.) Risk in business is acceptable, but risk in government is discouraged. Governmental agencies usually take the most conservative route—thereby taking important options off the table.

As a rule, government agencies generally give too much control to lawyers. They have a role—indeed an important one—but they are *not* policy makers. You are. Don't let lawyers shunt your creativity or your ability to think outside the box. Lawyers often like to tell you what you can't do. That's the easy route. An exceptional lawyer will find out what you want to do and find a legal way to help you accomplish your goals.

The "culture of can't" can stifle creative solutions to problems. Timid, risk-free government is static and ineffectual. New ideas and new ways of doing things energize people and can lead to improvements in service or efficiency. Calculated risks are necessary, although, in truth, they don't always lead to success. And when things don't work out it is important that elected officials stand up and take the blame or responsibility. It is a rare quality, and part of assessing risk.

There is another element of risk taking that we talk about later in this book, but it is worth mentioning here as well. The well-documented scandals in Bell and Vernon, California, were not caused by one or two unsavory people. The thievery (in these instances, extraordinary salaries and pensions given to elected officials and public "servants" and the steering of city contracts to friends and families of elected officials) was not committed in the dead of night by masked anonymous individuals. The theft was committed in the light of day, at public or semi-public meetings, with the support or tacit approval of other council members and staff. These were not innocent errors. The thieves were people elected or hired to protect the public interests.

A series of investigative stories written by *Los Angeles Times* reporters Jeff Gottlieb and Ruben Vives starting on July 15, 2010, revealed that several city officials were being paid salaries significantly higher than those in other cities. For example, Bell's city manager, Robert Rizzo, collected a salary of $787,637 a year, with yearly 12 percent increases scheduled every July, receiving $1.5 million in his last year of employment. (The U.S. president only makes $400,000 annually!) Rizzo also received an unusually large package of benefits, including paid vacation, sick, and personal leave of twenty-eight weeks off per year. In addition, he was in line to receive a pension of $880,000 annually before the story broke.

As noted in another *Los Angeles Times* article by Corina Knoll on July 16, 2010, what made matters worse was that Bell is a very small town, covering 2.5 square miles near Los Angeles, with a population of approximately 38,000. It is one of the poorest cities in Los Angeles County, with almost one in six residents living below the poverty line. The per capita income in 2009 was about $24,800. Roughly 90 percent of residents are Hispanic; many do not have a high school education.

Small businesses, auto shops, markets, *carnicerias* (butcher shops), and *panaderias* (bakeries) dominate the streets of the small town, and Bell's unemployment level is 16 percent.

According to a follow-up *Los Angeles Times* story by Sam Allen and Hector Becerra on September 9, 2010, nearby in the City of Vernon, the smallest city in California with 112 residents, the city manager received an astounding $1.6 million annual salary with some fancy perks, including first-class air travel around the world and $800-a-night hotel rooms.

In both Bell and Vernon, many people were aware that what was going on didn't pass the "smell test," but they didn't speak up. Why didn't people speak up? Perhaps they were afraid of the risk of speaking up. It took an investigative reporter to uncover this story. That is part of the tragedy.

In your desire to work cooperatively with other elected officials or staff, it may be difficult to speak up when you feel something is wrong. It may be especially hard if you are benefiting as well. Entitlement is not a benefit of office. If you or your colleagues are doing something that crosses a legal or ethical line it hurts everyone. It is an even bigger problem if you keep your mouth shut if you see something wrong. Yes, there is risk. You may fear being shunned by your colleagues or fear confronting others and exposing something that could embarrass them, and you.

Does a fellow board member pad his expenses? Is a colleague taking excessive travel on the public's dime? Is the trip to a conference, paid for by taxpayers, really an excuse for a vacation paid for by taxpayers? Are there hidden benefits for a privileged few that the public doesn't see or know about?

Your colleagues may be friends or allies or even effective members of the board. But if you notice unethical behavior, are you willing to take the risk of exposing them? Handling these situations is not easy. But that does not mean they should be ignored or condoned. Here are some suggestions for dealing with these difficult and sensitive situations:

Step one: In private, inform your colleague he or she may be doing something improper. Tell the person what it is and why. Step two: Speak to the head of your agency, city manager, city attorney, or superintendent of schools (unless, of course, they are the ones you are confronting). In most cases you will not need to take a step three. But if you do, put your comments in writing and ask to discuss them in closed session with legal counsel.

© 2012 Tom Meyer

Self Reflection

What are the things that you want to accomplish that will involve taking some risk?

_____

_____

How important are these things to you and the community?

_____

_____

How will the community benefit if you are willing to take the risk and are successful?

_____

_____

Who will be supportive? Who will be opposed?

_____

_____

How do you evaluate the level of risk?

_____

_____

What are the political implications of your actions?

_____

_____

CHAPTER THIRTEEN
Finding balance/setting limits

"One has to find a balance between what people need from you and what you need for yourself."

Jessye Norman, world-famous opera singer

I recently sent surveys to elected officials asking them what the toughest things about being elected were. The two most common answers: "Having balance between public life and private life," and "Finding the time necessary to be effective." Some went so far as to say that it was impossible to have a balanced life once you are elected. If you want a balanced life or free time, they cautioned, stay out of politics.

Personal and professional balance is difficult to achieve in any demanding profession. In politics or government, the lines between personal life and professional responsibilities are blurry to say the least. And unlike state and federal officials, who are able to escape to state capitals or to Washington, D.C., local officials have no place to hide. The people that serve at the local level are in daily contact with the people who elect them. Social events can easily become political events, and elected officials are expected to be "on duty" all the time. A school board member is likely to be questioned at a soccer game about test scores or the performance of a particular teacher. A city council member may be at the grocery store or the dentist, but that doesn't stop someone from asking about streetlights or crime.

For elected officials, having balance may be more about setting boundaries. No one we interviewed has the "right" answer that will work for everyone. Setting limits and having relationships and activities outside of political friendships and political activities were commonly suggested practices to help maintain a private life.

Finding balance is an individual challenge for each person. When Aristotle argued that government (the city-state) existed for the attainment of the "good life" 2,400 years ago, he was referring to the good life of the broader public, not his own good life or that of a public leader. My guess is he knew a public leader had to make sacrifices, and one of those sacrifices was privacy.

Today, having a private life and a political life, for most elected officials, seems incompatible. It is difficult, if not impossible, to tune out or turn off. With email, smart phones, electronic notices and updates, and the demand to multitask, privacy is very difficult to achieve for anyone in public office. Official meetings, committees, special sessions, negotiating sessions, community outreach, task forces, constituent meetings (let alone the additional things we recommend doing, like continuing to do door-to-door work) all demand significant time and attention. For local elected officials, most of whom have no staff to help them, there aren't enough hours in the day. And while our days have as many hours in them as days did in Aristotle's time, the daily demands of public officials greatly exceed those of classical Athens.

Here are the best practices gathered from elected officials on how to set limits:

- Find something else that you are interested in that takes you away from your work. Take the time to pursue that activity. Don't feel obligated to talk about politics or government or the issue of the day.

- Stay off your iPhone or BlackBerry. (How hard is this? Very hard.) Disconnecting, at least for some time daily, is essential. Resist the temptation to check emails. (Yes, we know it's hard!)

- Remember you are not as important as you think you are. You are not indispensable or irreplaceable. People served in your position before you and others will serve after you. If you need to miss a meeting, the world won't stop. Most people don't even know who you are. Don't believe this is true? Stand on the busiest intersection in your town or in the shopping mall. Don't wear a button or carry a sign. Ask one hundred people who pass by, "Who is the elected representative for [your position]?" You will be shocked how many people don't know you exist.

- Restrict the number of meetings/events/fund-raisers you attend. Always ask yourself, "Is this meeting essential?" Every day of the week could be spent in a meeting or many meetings. While some are essential and required, many can be eliminated. Be selective.

- Get others to help you do your job. Micki Winkler, a former council member from Menlo Park, kept her balance by involving other people (volunteers) in helping her. "Ideally, each elected official, or pair of elected officials, should have a team of residents (the proverbial kitchen cabinet) that will work with them during their course of office. Team members can be focused on general issues or specific topics. Their job is to ferret out and question the underlying assumptions of the staff reports." These volunteers were essential in helping Micki keep on top of issues.

- A supportive spouse or partner is critical. Balancing family needs will take joint effort and good communication. If your spouse is not supportive or, even worse, critical of the time you spend as an elected official, you will have problems. Take time every week to discuss schedules, responsibilities, and commitments. Good communication is essential.

- Develop friendships that are based on things other than politics. Develop friends who don't care that you are an elected official. Take a look at your friends. Would they still be your friends if you weren't an elected official? Would they return your calls if you were out of office? Do you have anything in common other than government or politics? If you answered "no" to any of these questions, you may have a problem of balance. More importantly, you are going to be very alone when you leave office, and staying in office because you have no outside interests is absolutely the last reason to be in office.

- Avoid being buttonholed at the grocery store or soccer games by constituents who want to bend your ear. Carry ten to fifteen self-addressed, stamped postcards. When constituents want to talk, hand them a postcard. Tell them, "I really don't have time right now to talk. But write me a note and send it to me and I will get back to you." Most people will understand, and you don't have to feign interest when you are picking out tomatoes. Being accessible is part of what makes local government unique. Make it work for you.

133

Ken Nordoff, city manager of Walnut Creek, California, observes, "In today's high-tech, high-touch, always 'on' approach to governing, my opinion is that elected officials, now more than ever, need to find a balance. Unfortunately, our DNA makes it extremely difficult to shut down. Strategies need to include days/weeks of unavailability (block them out on your calendar), taking deliberate vacations (out of cell phone reach), or pursuing other interests and hobbies. For many years, Walnut Creek utilized a 'city council break' whereby we have no second meeting in August, nor first meeting in September. At least two benefits come from this: The staff knows this in advance, and can adjust our workload accordingly. It also allows intentional time for family vacation and other interests that are accommodated around the work of city government."

Mary Jo Zenk, author of *The 7 Keys to Unlocking the Secrets of Your City's Budget*, gives these tips to elected officials. "My husband was a city council member when we lived back East. It was a very small town and he couldn't even cut the lawn or do any work on our house without getting into some discussion with a neighbor who was passing by. It is important to make time for yourself and your family and not always be available. You will get burnt out quickly and so will your family. Give yourself one or two nights a week that you are not available for city business. Keep a separate email account and possibly a cell phone for your city business and don't give out your personal email and phone."

Recognizing the symptoms of imbalance can be an important first step to recovery. Do any of these signs sound familiar to you?

- You have a hard time going fifteen or twenty minutes without checking your email.

- You have become short with people, including your family, friends, and colleagues.
- You are not interested in reading anything for pleasure.
- You think you are indispensable.
- You can't think of anything to do when you have free time.
- You don't have free time.
- You have a drink or two to take the edge off.
- You don't have any friends outside of work.
- The only friends you have are people who want your company because you are an elected official.
- You spend no time on other interests beyond those required of being an elected official.

Joseph P. Riley, Jr., has been mayor of Charleston, South Carolina, for thirty-six years and is in his tenth term as mayor. One of America's longest-serving mayors, Mayor Riley is also regarded as one of America's best mayors. In an article in the *New York Times*, reporter Kim Stevenson says that the secret to Mayor Riley's success may rest in his decision not to take work home.

"The mayor does not take work home, preferring a simple dinner and perhaps a good book on history. He tries to keep weekends free, too, limiting the numbers of banquets and parades he attends. 'To be an effective leader and have energy, you need time for repose,' he said. 'My citizens want me to have a clear head and have energy and be fresh and be creative and not become a robot or some machine that goes around shaking hands and attends everything.'"

Remember, finding balance takes effort. You will need to keep at it.

What will *you* do to set limits? Remember, you are unique. What works for someone else may not work for you.

© 2012 Tom Meyer

Self Reflection

List the things you will do to set limits. You should review this list every month to make sure you're on track. Write your list here:

1. _____

_____

2. _____

_____

3. _____

_____

Who are individuals in your life that you can connect with who are not associated with your political life?

_____

_____

CHAPTER FOURTEEN

Turning problems into opportunities

"Problems are only opportunities in work clothes."

Henry J. Kaiser, American industrialist and philanthropist

Chicago Mayor Rahm Emmanuel, who is a veteran of the rough-and-tumble world of politics, is quoted as saying, "Never let a serious crisis go to waste." A crisis provides opportunities to improve and do things in a new way. A public safety crisis may trigger improvements in the way emergency services are provided. A financial crisis may force an agency to rethink budget priorities and to reassess personnel and other costs that once seemed untouchable. The loss of a key individual through retirement or resignation may allow others to assume new responsibilities or prompt reorganization of a job function.

Twenty-five years ago, California's once vaunted public school system was facing a crisis. Schools, built decades earlier, were inadequate for a growing and changing student population. In thousands of schools electrical systems were inadequate and unsafe, classrooms were cramped (some schools even used storage rooms and closets for classrooms), and technology consisted of one electrical outlet and an overhead projector. In short, school facilities were woefully out-of-date. The list of problems was endless and the needed renovations expensive. By any definition, public schools in California were in a crisis.

Without waiting for the state government to provide funds, school leaders worked community by community to convince local taxpayers to support local tax measures (requiring 66.7 percent voter approval for passage!) to provide local funds to build and renovate schools. Thousands of schools across the state were renovated and hundreds of new schools were built.

140

In time, these same school leaders worked successfully to pass a statewide ballot measure to reduce the threshold for passing school bonds to 55 percent. The result of these efforts was a massive taxpayer investment in school and college facilities. Thousands of people were employed, and local economies benefited as billions of dollars were spent on the renovation efforts. But the biggest beneficiaries were the children who finally had adequate, safe instructional facilities.

Out of crisis came opportunity. These local school leaders did not wait for those in higher office to solve their problems. They took action, small at first. One district, then another attempted a bond measure. Over time, school districts throughout the state were evaluating their own needs. California, the largest state in the nation, began solving one of the biggest problems—adequate educational facilities—by starting one district at a time. Today, it is a rare California school district that has not taken steps to upgrade local schools. And, it wasn't the state government, but local leaders, that made it happen.

What are other crises that may provide opportunities?

Could the pension crisis lead to significant reform?

Could the financial crisis lead to a new way of cities providing for and paying for services?

Could the stagnant economy force cities to look at new ways to attract and create jobs?

Could the cost of oil and gasoline lead to changes in transportation and infrastructure?

During your term of office, something unexpected is likely to happen—an earthquake perhaps, or a flood, a tornado, or maybe a massive fire. It may not be a natural disaster. Perhaps a colleague passes away or some key person in government leaves or becomes severely ill. Downturns in the economy, strikes, civil disobedience, and labor disputes can create crises that will need to be managed. A crisis can lead to opportunity, and the people who handle the crisis effectively are those best prepared.

Dianne Feinstein rose to national prominence in 1978 after her adept handling of the crisis when San Francisco Mayor George Moscone and Supervisor Harvey Milk were assassinated. No one outside of her close family and friends could have predicted Feinstein's grace under fire and competence during this time of enormous stress and pressure. Feinstein, who was president of the board of supervisors at the time, is credited with rallying the city during a difficult period. Her popularity and eventual election to the U.S. Senate was due in no small part to her leadership and her ability to manage a crisis no one could have predicted.

When a disaster occurs at the national level, we expect our elected leaders (usually the president) to show courage and compassion, to be present, and to take appropriate and effective action to deal with the crisis. At the local level, the elected officials are not expected to take charge in the same way. With few exceptions, managing these crises is the responsibility of the people who are hired, not elected.

How will you respond when there is a major crisis? What is your role? Unless you are an elected mayor of a city that has a "strong mayor" form of government, you probably won't have much of a role. Let the people responsible handle it. The primary responsibility of an elected official is to stay out of the way and make sure the crisis is handled appropriately. Your work occurred earlier, to prepare a plan with procedures and policies to follow in a crisis. Hopefully, these crisis plans were developed well before the crisis occurred.

Many observers of the Occupy Wall Street movement noticed how differently various cities and elected officials handled the demonstrations. The cities that handled the demonstrations appropriately had contingency plans developed ahead of time so that decisions could be made calmly and thoughtfully, not in the heat of the battle. The rights of the demonstrators, as well as businesses and the public, were protected. In other cities, decisions were made, and then reversed, then reversed again, revealing the fact that there was no thoughtful crisis management plan. As a result, everyone, including demonstrators, police, citizens, and businesses, became angry and lost faith in their city leaders.

As a crisis unfolds, elected officials should make sure the people responsible for crisis management are following protocols. After the fact, you need to make sure the procedures that were set up prior to the crisis were followed and use the opportunity to make changes or improvements in the plan.

Jonathan Daugherty cautions, "The best thing you can do in a crisis is stay out of the way. We have police chiefs and city managers that are trained to handle a crisis. By showing up in a situation like this, you are only preventing them from doing their job. Remember, by yourself you have absolutely no power or authority. You must get a majority vote of your commission or council to do anything. Many of the lower level employees do not realize this, though, and often an elected official will try to take a leadership role in a crisis situation and only disrupt the proper chain of command. You do not want to get into the habit of micromanaging your city. Let your department heads do their jobs."

Rod Gould adds that while everyday needs often take precedence, emergency preparedness often gets lost in difficult budgetary times. Elected officials need to make sure that funds are set aside for emergencies and to ask for periodic updates.

Opportunities and problems caused by elections

New people, new energy, and new ideas are brought into government through elections. These elections every two or four years create institutional change that creates opportunities (as well as new problems).

Candidates seeking voter support often identify opportunities because they are not encumbered with the realities of office. Where others see a dump, they may see a park. Where others may see an abandoned store, they may see the potential for a senior center or a youth center. Elections provide a new start, a fresh look at problems, a time for proposing new solutions.

But elections can also have negative impacts. Changes in the makeup of a local elected board can also cause disruption and create new challenges. An election where incumbents, or some of them, are not re-elected and new members now take their places can wreak havoc on a formerly well-functioning board. Michael Conduff, consultant to cities and government and former city manager of Bryan, Texas, warns that in these situations the incumbent members need to recognize that a new board exists and that new members may not only have new ideas but they may also have "differing values, dissimilar objectives, or downright opposing views."

Change in the composition of an elected board may disrupt plans and projects. Newly elected officials eager to make a difference may not be aware of how long a specific issue has been simmering, or they may lack the background to appreciate its complexity. Complicated issues may take years to be resolved. Experienced board members will need to mentor the newer members on the history and context of some of the difficult issues.

A school district was in the midst of a long-anticipated and expensive school modernization project. A newly elected board member was critical of the way he felt money was being spent. Although voters had previously approved the projects and the expenditures, the new board member asked for new reports and briefings on all projects, slowing the renovation and adding to expensive delays. The superintendent, the business manager, and the construction manager of the district patiently spent weeks briefing the new board member and eventually the renovations got back on track.

Two years later, the formerly "new" board member, now "seasoned," admitted he had made mistakes when he was first elected. "A new broom," he said, "sometimes does not sweep clean, it just makes a mess! I thought I knew a whole lot more when I was first elected than I really did."

Conduff describes this learning process: "Just think how long it takes to tackle a significant public project such as revitalizing a downtown, establishing a business park or retail center, or beginning a relatively straightforward infrastructure improvement. It seems we no sooner get past the public engagement component, the significant policy debate, and the consensus development, then we have a new set of 'players' without the institutional history or commitment to the project."

Experienced board members, as well as agency staff, need to seize the opportunity and the obligation to mentor the newer members, recognizing that the world has changed and that the new members may now represent the current views of the public, or at least some of the public. New board members need to respect that they are now part of a team and that it will take time to get up to speed.

Problems create opportunities. The effort made in tackling problems is where the effective elected official makes a difference. The only reason to be elected, or perhaps the only *good* reason, is to tackle problems that face your community.

A crisis caused by overdevelopment may lead to a more environmentally friendly city council.

Conversely, a shrinking tax base may force a city to think about ways to attract more businesses and development.

During the 1950s the polio crisis spurred a national effort for vaccines and the building of community hospitals around the country.

Today, schools and colleges are responding to the need for students to become more proficient in math and science by offering more courses and developing higher standards.

Fires can prompt renewed efforts to promote fire safety and improve emergency systems.

Like the school facility crisis in California, it is likely that the solutions to persistent problems will come from the local level, not from the state government or the federal government. Local elected officials, if they are willing to seize opportunities, are in a great position to lead and make the difference they envisioned when running for office.

Self Reflection

Does your agency have a disaster management plan?

_____

_____

Do you know what your responsibilities will be in the event of a crisis?

_____

_____

What crises do you see on the horizon? What opportunities?

_____

_____

Do you have a team that can help you analyze and make sense of a crisis?

_____

_____

Do you have a process in place to consider lessons learned?

_____

_____

CHAPTER FIFTEEN

New media, old media.
Getting the coverage you want.

© 2012 Tom Meyer

"Twitter is a great place to tell the world what you're thinking before you had a chance to think about it."

Chris Pirillo, blogger

Elected officials often have a love/hate relationship with the press. They want coverage (favorable, of course), and they obsess when the coverage is not to their liking. They want attention and publicity when things go well, but they want to be left alone when things do not. Most elected officials want to develop a working relationship with the people who write about local news, and they should.

Developing a good relationship with the people who report on local issues is important, but it is not easy. Nevertheless, every person elected to local office needs to have a strategy on how to get information out to the public. The press, in all of its various forms (including bloggers), can be important and helpful if you know what it can and can't do. Developing a strategy to communicate directly with the public must be part of your overall communication strategy.

With the decline in readership of daily newspapers, local issues are being squeezed out of the news. Newspaper reporters today have broader responsibilities and cover larger areas, so it is unlikely that local issues will even make the news. For an elected official it can be frustrating when you are not able to get coverage of issues you believe are worthy, like the closing (or opening) of a firehouse or your efforts to deal with the budget deficit.

Despite being in the Information Age, the information available to most people regarding local issues is pretty meager. Fifty years ago, people received their news mostly from a local newspaper or the local radio station. Twenty years ago, from TV. Today, more and more people, if they receive news at all, probably get it online where they have the ability to select the news they are interested in and ignore news that does not interest them.

As the manner people receive their news today changes, it becomes even more difficult to "manage" the press or to even know what information people are getting. Blogs, social media, smart phones, and smart pads have changed the way people receive and respond to news. "News" shows are often more about celebrities or entertainment than news. (The latest news on a Kardashian marriage will receive more interest than efforts to revitalize the local school district.)

People who report local news generally fit into a number of broad categories.

First are the reporters who work at smaller local newspapers, usually weeklies. Many of these reporters are young and inexperienced and can present a challenge, because some may not have the broad background or needed perspective. Others, however, may have been involved in the community for years and know a lot about many issues. Do you know the difference? Have you taken the time to find out?

The second category includes reporters who choose to cover local issues and often work for larger newspapers or news outlets. These reporters are assigned to cover issues that have some real importance or controversy and also may know more about what is going on than the elected officials. In some communities, these reporters have been around many years. Sometimes the newspaper or news agency designates a reporter to cover a particular beat, say the city council, the school district, or the hospital district. While these reporters do not generally write editorials, they are very influential because of their knowledge and experience. Who is assigned to your beat? What do you know about them?

A third type may work for alternative newspapers with a clearly defined political perspective. While some reporters are fair and balanced, some reporters for weekly alternative newspapers mix fact and opinion in an effort to bolster a particular point of view. What is their point of view? Is it worthwhile to engage?

Fourth are reporters who cover national or regional news, but because a local story has turned into a national story, they are now reporting on the local issue. (The fiasco in the City of Bell in 2011 is one example.) Reporters assigned to these issues generally are not interested in the nuances of your city or what you are trying to do. They are there to cover the big story, and they get out of town as quickly as they came in.

Finally, there are the growing number of bloggers and self-appointed reporters who write about local issues but do not (generally) have formal journalistic backgrounds. While they may lack journalistic training, many have developed a following among insiders who get their news electronically and who themselves contribute to ongoing online discussions. Who are the people who blog on local issues? How significant is their following? Do they mix fact and opinion? Pay attention to these news sources.

Elected officials need to develop a working relationship with the people reporting the local news, all of them. You need to know with whom you are dealing and what *their* motivations or political perspectives are.

Most reporters want to be fair. However, in striving to be balanced, a reporter may give the other side more credibility than it deserves. Don't worry about it. If you feel they are wrong or misinformed, let them know politely. Take the time to give them additional facts or your perspective if you feel they are wrong. They will respect you. Most reporters want to deal with fact, not opinion.

As a rule, elected officials are often more concerned about press coverage than they should be. One story does not an issue make. It is easy to become obsessed with newspaper coverage, especially if it is not to your liking. Rarely, however, is the coverage in a newspaper or a blog overly important one way or another. Local issues are likely to be buried somewhere in the second section of the newspaper between the comics and the horoscopes. Don't obsess about it. Your success as an elected official will rarely be affected by press coverage—good, bad, or nonexistent.

Here are some tips for dealing with **old media**:

- Reporters often say they are on deadline. This can be a tactic to get you to talk to them. Their deadline is not your deadline. Deal with reporters when *you* are ready and available. On the other hand, if you want to get something out, and the deadline is real, you will have to talk sooner than later. They may, in fact, really be on deadline.

- Reporters deserve a call back. Find out what they want to talk about so you are prepared.

- It's perfectly acceptable, and often a good idea, to ask the reporter to email you his or her questions so you can respond online. This gives you a little more time to craft your answers without being taken off guard by a phone call during a hectic morning. It can help you avoid being misquoted, too!

- Anyone who says he or she is an expert in dealing with the press usually isn't.

- Nothing is ever off the record. Nothing.

- Never say "No comment." Ever. You will be quoted that way and it will look like you're hiding something.
- The farther away the reporter gets from a pad and pencil and the closer to a camera, the more superficial the coverage.
- Never allow your spouse to speak to the press, especially if it is in response to something negative. (Politics is business; it is not personal.)
- Be straightforward. Spinning doesn't work unless you are an ice skater or on an exercise bike.
- If you don't know the answer to a question, tell the reporter you will get back to her.
- Get back to her.
- News articles rarely make or break anything. Take them in stride.
- If you feel you have been quoted inaccurately or a story is inaccurate, call the reporter only when you have chilled out and can speak calmly. Calling the reporter won't do much good, but you might feel better.
- Editorial writers have less influence than they think they have. (Observation: most people don't read editorials, and those that do usually have their minds made up already.)
- Unless a story was in the news for days on end, there is a great chance few people saw it.
- Articles that appear in the newspaper are more closely read by insiders than by the public in general. Don't assume that because an article was in the newspaper anyone read it.
- Balancing your desire to get good press for yourself individually with your responsibility to your colleagues with

whom you serve can be difficult at times. Board members who routinely go to the press or publicly air grievances rarely do themselves or their agency any good.

- Writing letters to the editor or submitting an op-ed column is a good way to add more to a story than was covered. Most papers have a word maximum and limit the number of times they run letters from writers, so pick your battles! Letters to the editor are one of the most popular sections of a newspaper and an important public relations tool that is often underutilized by elected officials.

- While letters to the editor provide a forum for getting the word out, don't fret when a letter appears that opposes your viewpoint. Few people change their opinions based on a letter to the editor. No campaign was ever won or lost because of letters to the editor.

- When you speak to the press, don't guess on answers to questions. You will gain far more credibility by acknowledging that you do not know or are not sure. It is better to be factual than make an educated guess and perhaps be wrong.

- If you are not appointed as the official spokesperson or the designated spokesperson for your agency, you must not speak for the agency. You are just one of a number of elected officials.

The new media

Mark Twain's old quote "Never pick a fight with someone who buys ink by the barrel" may have outlived its usefulness. As fewer and fewer people purchase ink by the barrel, the dissemination of information/news has become more diverse and less controlled by the journalistic elite. Blogs, Facebook, and Twitter have more followers and more readers than many newspapers. In fact, today there are more people on Facebook than were on the planet two hundred years ago. Anyone who wants to influence public opinion must take advantage of these new media sources.

New York City Mayor Michael Bloomberg, who has more than 230,000 followers on Twitter and who uses social media as aggressively as anyone in office, cautions that social media tends to give voice to naysayers and make long-term improvements more difficult. Every project, every proposal can become controversial.

In an article in the *New York Times* on March 22, 2012, Mayor Bloomberg observes, "We are basically having a referendum on every single thing that we do every day. And it is very hard for people to stand up to that and say, 'No, no this is what we're going to do,' when there is constant criticism." Mayor Bloomberg is quoted as saying long-term urban planning "requires leadership and standing up and saying, 'You know, you elected me, this is what we're going to do,' and not take a referendum on every single thing."

In the past, leaders took "to the stump" to push new ideas or to build support for new programs. Today, new media or social media can reach far more people, far quicker. One cannot avoid it; one has to become a master at using it.

Here are some of the best ideas on dealing with new media:

- There is no longer one source for news. Get connected and work them all to get your message out. Social media consultants can get you started if you aren't taking advantage of these tools yet.

- Know who your audience is and make sure you are posting information that piques their interest.
- Keep most of your communications short.
- Don't take seriously or respond to the outlandish comments posted by people.
- Inject your personality into your posts, profiles, and various pages. To be effective, your social media outreach will have to be personal.
- Calls to action should be teed up with informative posts/emails that segue into your "ask," or they should provide background information about why your issue is important.
- Respond to questions and positively engage with people who follow your postings.
- Don't operate your social media separately from your overall press strategy—they must be interconnected to be effective.
- Don't bore people with all the details of your life. Be personal sparingly, but be professional.
- Continually ask people for input, ideas, and suggestions on how to improve local government.

With all the talk about new media, old media, the importance of good press coverage, or how to respond to bad press coverage, we often forget the *best* media is one you control. You have the ability to communicate directly with the public, your constituents, and your supporters through newsletters (both electronic and printed) and through direct mail.

A city council member publishes a "Neighborhood Report" six times a year and distributes the report throughout her council district door to door with volunteers. Each newsletter covers current issues in the city, and the efforts of the councilwoman and local events are featured. This easy-to-produce newsletter is recognized as an important news source about the city, the councilwoman, and the community. The key to the success of these newsletters is repetition and consistency.

When you feel the need to complain about the press, evaluate your own efforts to communicate to the public. What are you doing to communicate? What is your plan?

© 2012 Tom Meyer

Self Reflection

Who are the reporters that cover the local issues? What do you know about them?

_____

_____

Who are the bloggers or online news sites that cover local issues?

_____

_____

How are you taking advantage of social media?

_____

_____

How are you providing opportunities for two-way communication?

_____

_____

CHAPTER SIXTEEN

Dealing with ideologues and disrupters

© 2012 Tom Meyer

"A fanatic is one who can't change his mind and won't change the subject."

Winston Churchill

I have a good friend who jokes that the majority, if not all, of the people who attend city council meetings or school board meetings on a regular basis fall into one of three categories: "People elected to be there, paid to be there, or . . . crazy."

While that may be somewhat of an exaggeration, anyone who regularly attends public meetings will see the same people again and again and again. Some may have a special cause that they want to publicize. Some speak on every issue at every meeting. Some just want attention. Some have nothing else to do.

It is a rare public entity that doesn't have one or two gadflies who take every opportunity to use the council meeting to air their opinions, relevant or not. Public comment periods provide opportunities to harangue, embarrass, or belittle elected officials and staff.

It is not just the occasional gadfly who can disrupt meetings. Special interest groups (representing all degrees of the political spectrum) have become adept at mobilizing their troops to attempt to influence public officials. During budget negotiations, for example, an interest group may organize to disrupt proceedings as a show of force to intimidate or persuade elected officials. The more controversial the issue, the more likely it will happen. Since meetings of public entities are not generally well attended, a show of force by an interest group is intended to create the impression that the whole community is watching.

Keep your cool. Listen to the facts and don't overreact. Public demonstrations are a necessary component of public discourse, but rarely do they contribute to quality decision making.

Occasionally, an issue sparks intense public interest. But even when public opinion is evenly divided, the people who are motivated to attend meetings are usually the opponents of whatever action is contemplated. A proposal for a new store may trigger opposition from the competition or neighbors who fear traffic or disruption. Proposals to build a new wing on a school will bring out neighbors who fear the loss of open space. Union members may pack a meeting during negotiations. Cutbacks in school budgets always attract parents and teachers, eager to save programs or jobs. Employees who are affected by the changes in a new contract are more likely to appear than members of the public, who will ultimately pay for the costs negotiated in a new contract.

The people who pack a room at any specific time may or may not represent the best interests of the community or even the will of the community. An elected official must have the strength to make decisions that benefit the entire community, not those who are the loudest, those who are the better organized, or the ones who attend the meetings. A public official represents everyone. Balancing the various needs of the community is one of the most difficult jobs of being an elected official.

It is easy for an elected official, especially when he or she is the target of a verbal assault or demonstration, to become frustrated and even angry with people who speak at public meetings. It is just as easy for an elected official to pander to the crowd. Neither approach contributes to good government.

Some city councils have tried various strategies to keep order. The city council in Carlsbad, California, frustrated by an individual who continued to use "inappropriate language" at council meetings, tried to limit public speech by passing an ordinance that prohibited vulgar or profane speech at public meetings. The tipping point for the council came when a homeless man repeatedly used a word that some consider a vulgar reference to a female body part during a city council meeting. The speaker was pulled from the public speakers' podium and arrested. He then sued the city seeking to overturn the city's codes regarding conduct at public meetings. The ACLU joined the case, journalists weighed in, and the result was increased legal expenses for the city and public embarrassment for all. As you might expect, the incident and the city's reaction to it created publicity well beyond the importance of the issue.

How could this have been handled differently? Carlsbad resident, attorney, and council-watcher Leon Page suggests: "Turn the other cheek. Let them ramble. It looks far worse (and is far more dangerous from a risk management perspective) to stomp on the speaker's First Amendment rights."

Gary Neely adds, "Give the public (whoever it is) a reasonable amount of time to say what they came to the meeting to say and make the effort to at least look like you are hearing what they're saying. Most people aren't chronic malcontents. The quickest way to change that percentage is by treating people's opinions with disdain, condescension, or contempt the first time they find their way to the public microphone. An hour invested in listening to people 'vent' will ultimately save you from hundreds of hours of mind-numbing legalese and pontificating before all has been said and done."

It is not just the disrupters who impede progress. In every community there are naysayers and people who will oppose even the most benign improvement or change, citing any number of excuses— cost, time, or inconvenience, just to mention a few. The easiest path is to do nothing.

Rod Gould of Santa Monica cautions, "It is important for elected officials to know the difference between real public opinion and the chatter of the noisemakers in the community. There are just certain individuals and groups that communicate a whole lot more often and louder than the great majority of constituents. Often what seems to be a disgruntled electorate according to letters to the editor and blogs is really a pluralistic community that in general is quite satisfied."

A respected city manager, in an extremely candid moment, reflected that it was his experience that the worst disrupters of the legislative process, and the people who waste most of the public's resources, are the ideologues and naysayers on both sides of the political spectrum. Unfortunately, these ideologues, according to the city manager, can oftentimes be elected officials, who regardless of fact or necessity refuse to compromise or to work to find solutions to problems.

In local government where there are only five, at most seven, elected members on a board, one person who refuses to compromise or follow the rules, who pushes ideology over practicality, can cause tremendous disruption. The effective elected official must be willing to listen and to accommodate differing opinions, perspectives, and interests. The power in local office is a collective power. It is shared with fellow elected officials and with the public. It may be necessary, at times, to compromise on something in order to move an initiative forward. Ideologues rarely make good elected leaders or community leaders.

Ideologues look at compromise as failure, but compromise is what legislative action and government is all about. A skillful elected leader learns what is essential to each of his/her colleagues so solutions can be reached.

Throughout this book we have talked about balance. Balancing responsibilities of office with personal life; balancing the various needs of the community; balancing differing opinions. Ideologues, naysayers, and even disrupters all have an important role in a democracy. They need to be respectfully listened to. There may be truth, even wisdom, in what the ideologues have to say. At the same time, your job is to find balance and to lead. This is done through building relationships and compromise.

An activist often has difficulty adapting to the new role. One former activist who ran successfully for office told me: "As a citizen I attended a few council meetings to express my opinion. I always felt that those making decisions were sellouts. Now that I am elected I see the need to balance many different perspectives and priorities. I've learned that my most effective colleagues are those who are able to forge compromise and who are willing to sacrifice some of what they believe in for the greater good."

Self Reflection

How will you handle yourself when verbally attacked at a public meeting?

_____

_____

What polices has your agency adopted to balance the public's right to speak and the ability to conduct the public's business?

_____

_____

How can you make sure you are hearing all the facts?

_____

_____

How would you rate your skills at compromising?

_____

_____

CHAPTER SEVENTEEN
Avoiding the mistakes of others

© 2012 Tom Meyer

> *"All sins have their origin in a sense of inferiority,*
> *otherwise called ambition."*

Cesare Pavese, Italian author

Pick up any newspaper and it's possible you'll see an article about an elected official who is being criticized for taking a junket or using his or her influence to personal benefit. While they may be the exceptions, these instances are common enough not to seem extraordinary or unique. PublicCEO.com, a website devoted to news and information on local government, regularly posts articles that have been in the papers. One of the recent articles was about an elected official who had been charged with selling his vote to a developer to get support for a ballot measure that increased his salary as an elected official from $99,000 to more than $150,000 per year.

Another had to do with the scandal in the City of Vernon, California, where an elected official who pleaded guilty to corruption charges is still eligible to receive his pension from the state retirement system funded by taxpayers. His pension, which is the highest pension in the California Public Retirement System, is $509,664 per year!

$509,664 *PER YEAR* IN RETIREMENT! Forever? How did that happen? What public official makes that? Remember, Vernon is a city with a population of 112 people! What does information like this do to the public's perception of *all* elected officials?

Ethical behavior is not merely doing what is legal. Plenty of things are legal but not ethical. For elected officials, there must be a standard higher than merely doing what is legal.

It is not just elected officials in San Bernardino County who "hid the wolf in sheep's clothing" to raise their own salaries. In Oakland,

California, a number of years ago, the city council successfully placed a measure on the ballot that established an ethics commission. Sounds great, doesn't it? Who could be against ethics in government? No one. But the deal and details were in the fine print. The main motivation for creating the ethics commission was to have the ethics commission set the salaries of the city council members.

What did the ethics commission do in its first significant meeting? It raised the salaries of the council members who, not surprisingly, also fund and vote on the appointments to the ethics commission.

We tend to remember high-profile rogues and scoundrels like those in Bell or Vernon, California, or other elected officials who have been caught cheating or stealing in one manner or another. These cases of obvious greed or malfeasance gain headlines, but many officials on a daily basis are faced with less obvious ethical conflicts.

It is the acceptance of special things, sometimes gifts, sometimes perks, that can lead to bigger problems. While it may not lead elected officials down a road to corruption it may well affect how they look at themselves. At a minimum, the elected officials begin to believe they are special.

In an era defined by excesses and greed, some of the following things may seem small, but for elected officials they should be avoided. We like to call them the seven deadly sins of elected officials. Feel free to add your own.

Sin #1: Special perks and privileges.

High-profile cases of greed and malfeasance get a lot of attention. But public officials can also take advantage of their positions and power in small, seemingly insignificant ways. When it comes to ethical behavior, size doesn't matter.

Do you get things for free that no one else gets? It makes no difference if you are reporting these gifts on conflict of interest statements. If you are getting something for free because you are an elected official, it is wrong. Do you get free parking? (I'm not talking about a parking place at city hall, which could be excused.) Do you get free parking anywhere you park in the city? If you do, that's wrong. Do your parking tickets get fixed? That's wrong. Free parking at the airport in special lots? Don't accept it. Do you receive a pension for one term in office? You've got to be kidding.

Do you travel to a conference on the public's dime, but it's really a vacation? Are you really adding value to that delegation that is traveling overseas, or is it just an excuse for a free trip?

The problem with perks is that it takes self-discipline not to accept them (perhaps even antagonizing other elected colleagues if you don't), and most elected officials see nothing wrong in accepting perks, often rationalizing that everyone gets them. If you are getting for free what the average citizen has to pay for, it's wrong. Period. There doesn't have to be a law against it.

Sin #2: Thinking you are "above the law."

A council member has a placard that he places on his windshield that states, "Official Council Business." He uses it to park in red zones and handicapped zones at grocery stores and restaurants! A California state senator got caught speeding on a freeway. She tried to get off by saying she had a legitimate reason for breaking the law: she was late for a fund-raiser. A city council member, frustrated by the delay in getting a permit for a building he owned, contacted the head of the planning department to get expedited service. A city council member used her influence to have her son be one of the five (out of five hundred) applicants selected to attend the academy for firefighters.

Recently it was reported that members of Congress were exempt from conflict of interest rules for insider trading. Members of Congress, in both political parties, scrambled to deny, defend, or modify the rules. The fervor eventually died down, but there was little explanation why members of Congress were exempted in the first place.

A bit of power often emboldens elected leaders to bend or break rules to suit their personal or political needs. When politicians prove to be dishonest or less than ethical, we shrug our shoulders and think, "What's new?" Little or nothing is done about it. Elected officials put in lots of time and sacrifice a lot to serve their communities, but that does not entitle anyone to take advantage of the system.

Sin #3: Special favors for friends and families.

One of the worst things elected officials can do is to use their influence to help their own child or a friend. A city councilman's son was arrested for driving while intoxicated. Rather than face the music like anyone else, the councilman intervened with the police department to get the charges dropped. A school board member used her influence to get her daughter enrolled in a popular class that was already full, bumping another child who did not have a well-connected parent. A councilwoman put her boyfriend on the city budget as an aide despite the fact he never showed up for work. A city council member used his influence to get his son a summer job in the parks and recreation department.

Go back to chapter two. What was your reason to run for office? If it was to help family and friends, you have a problem. The role of a person on a city council or board is to set broad policy, not to provide constituent services or employment opportunities to friends or family.

Sin #4: Blaming others.

How refreshing it would be to hear an elected official say, "I wish I could have done more; I wish I could have done a better job." Rather, we hear all the reasons something hasn't been done, usually blaming others or saying that problems were outside of their control or responsibility. "It's the union's fault" or "The problem is [the economy, the state, my opponents]." Doing nothing, accomplishing nothing, is easy. Blaming something else or someone else is the easiest of all excuses. In local government there are always differing opinions and multiple ways to accomplish things. Blaming others for not accomplishing something says *you* were ineffective. *You* were unable to find solutions. Perhaps someone else will do better.

Effective elected leaders must be able to speak the truth, even when it may not be politically wise. This may mean even taking responsibility or blame when things do not go well. Re-election should be subordinate to serving wisely, courageously, and honestly.

Sin #5: Dogmatism/inability to compromise.

To make progress in government requires the ability to compromise. Occasionally an ideological purist gets elected. They make life miserable for their colleagues, and because of their inability to compromise, they rarely accomplish anything.

Even worse, they don't want others to be successful either. Adhering to their political ideology is more important than solving problems. These people are not confined to either the "left" or the "right." The paralysis we are experiencing in Washington and in state governments is in part due to the election of true believers who are more concerned about ideology than results. They would rather adhere to their own dogma (right or wrong) than to take steps to solve problems. At the local level, the inability to compromise can bring government to a halt.

Sin #6: Avoidance of tough problems.

Many problems are difficult to solve. Avoiding difficult problems because they are tough or complicated only kicks the can down the road. Can the city afford the generous pay raises and pensions of public employees that may have seemed acceptable during good economic times but are untenable today? Are the systems in place to evaluate superintendents, teachers, and principals? Is the city postponing a needed infrastructure improvement project because a tax increase would be necessary to fund it? Are incompetent employees terminated or are they merely reassigned somewhere else? If the city does not have the revenue to do all the things that are desired, what are the priorities? Has a process been set to establish priorities? What costs will be trimmed?

No problem is ever solved by avoidance. Avoidance of problems is always the easier strategy; it rarely is the best.

Sin #7: Arrogance.

Who among us hasn't noticed the change that occurs in people once they are elected? Winning an elective office can lead the best of people down a path toward arrogance. A parent who ran for office because she was concerned about the schools now believes she is an expert in school finance. The former union representative elected to city council is now lecturing business leaders on how they should run their businesses. The former city council aide who was appointed due to vacancy now lords over council meetings as though he was knighted. The council member without training, background, or expertise now lectures staff and the community on what is acceptable development.

The pinnacle of arrogance is the practice of public officials naming public facilities after themselves or their colleagues. Wouldn't it be refreshing to eliminate the practice of naming public facilities after elected officials, or at least wait until after some time has passed to determine their legacy? We now have state and federal buildings named for former elected officials, parks named after current members of city councils, open spaces named after legislators. Public service is public service. Naming a public facility after someone who sponsored a piece of legislation that provided funds for a project diminishes the role that many people played in the process. Naming public facilities after people should be reserved for real heroes, not elected officials.

Given how common the seven deadly sins are, and the inability of elected officials to recognize them in themselves, it is no surprise that there are attempts to legislate behavior. Term limits, once rare, are gaining supporters and are slowly becoming commonplace, even at the local level (usually due to citizen initiatives). The arguments on both sides of the debate are strong. Each community has to determine whether term limits would be an improvement or not.

New people can bring new energy and new ideas. Admittedly, some people stay in office way beyond their effectiveness. But term limits can also cut short the career of an effective leader, and turnover can wreak havoc with elected boards that operate well.

The worst reason to implement term limits is to get rid of the people that are currently in office. If the only way to get rid of incumbents is to limit their ability to run for office, there are probably bigger issues to be dealt with in the community. Why aren't other people running? Why do the current incumbents think they need to stay or be in office indefinitely? Implementing term limits should be something that is positive, not punitive. Don't be the reason your community decides to implement term limits.

The Kansas Leadership Center looked at leaders who made a difference, who were able to get things done despite enormous challenges. Written by Ed O'Malley, the following list (in italics) advises voters how to evaluate candidates. But the advice is so important, elected officials would do well to follow it.

Work across factions—*Progress on the deep, daunting issues requires elected officials to engage across the political spectrum from left to right. Talking about working across factions is easy. Actually doing it is different.*

Listen to all sides and seek out differing opinions. Worry less about electing a council majority who can dominate decision making. Work with those with whom you disagree.

Build a trustworthy process—*Facts and figures are fine, but trust greases the wheels of action in elected bodies. Do candidates have the trust of their colleagues? Do others from different political ideologies, while differing on policies, speak highly of a candidate's character?*

Your power only comes from the collective power of the board you sit on. You are not special. Working across ideological differences is the only way to make progress. Even to your opponents you need to be civil, kind, patient, supportive, and inclusive. What goes around comes around.

Infuse work with purpose—Too many elected officials lose sight of why they were elected. Effective civic leadership involves holding on relentlessly to purpose.

You were elected to do a job, not to have a job.

Be open to multiple interpretations—even uncomfortable ones. Question candidates' wisdom if they simply say Obama or Bush is to blame. Tough civic issues are complex, and politicians who simplify them with convenient scapegoats underestimate voters' discernment ability.

Accept responsibility. Period. No scapegoating or blaming others.

Speak to loss—Candidates who promote an "all gain and no pain" approach are misleading voters and perhaps even themselves. [Show] leadership . . . [by] acknowledging the downside to major policy changes. We need leadership, not just policy ideas and sound bites from elected officials.

Local government can't do everything. If we want more police officers we have to find a way to pay for them. If we want to reduce taxes we need to articulate what services will be lost. (We can't solve all budgets by just "cutting waste"!) Voters are smarter than we give them credit for. Give them options.

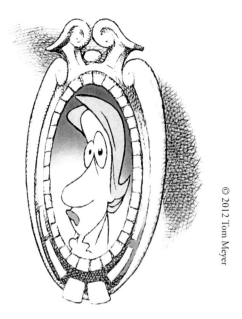

© 2012 Tom Meyer

Self Reflection

What perks do elected officials receive in your community? What would it take to eliminate these perks?

_____

_____

Have you ever used your official position to help a family member or a friend?

_____

_____

How willing are you to compromise? What issues are you unwilling to compromise?

_____

_____

179

Can you look in the mirror and say you haven't changed since you were elected? If you have changed, is it for the better?

_____

_____

CHAPTER EIGHTEEN

Your role after elected office

"Don't cry because it's over. Smile because it happened."

Dr. Seuss

Every community has problems. Some more than others. The problems that our elected leaders face today include crime, unemployment, underfunded education systems, inadequate healthcare, and environmental issues. These were problems that vexed elected officials a generation ago. The problems may be bigger and more complex today, but the challenges and problems are not new. Despite best efforts, they are likely to be problems that future generations and future elected officials will also have to deal with. Some of the problems will never be completely "solved." Other problems will also emerge.

When you were a candidate, solutions to problems may have seemed simpler. It may have seemed that these problems could be solved by electing better local leaders. As an elected official, you soon learn that solutions to difficult problems are complex and may take years to solve.

The difficulty or complexity of problems means little to the average citizen. Elected officials are the first people blamed when things don't go well. Lack of funding for schools may be a problem that was caused by state government or a downturn in revenue caused by a sluggish economy, but when your daughter's class had twenty-four students in a classroom last year and now has thirty-five, you take it out on the local school board member. When your car hits a pothole and is now out of alignment, you blame the ineptitude of local elected officials. When the police response to a burglary takes hours, not minutes, we blame our elected leaders for not hiring more police. Even when natural disasters, say fire or earthquakes, occur, it is the local elected officials who are looked to for help.

The one thing that makes serving in local government so exciting and important—the ability to solve problems—is also the most frustrating when you can't or don't. Because problems are so persistent and difficult to solve, there is a tendency to avoid them and to work on easier issues.

For persistent problems there are no magic fixes. A school district where students don't perform well may have numerous problems, each of which will take effort. The key to effective organizing, the key to change, and the key to being an effective elected leader is to start somewhere. The neighborhood watch program that you help establish may not curtail crime in all parts of the city, but it may make a big difference in a specific neighborhood. The efforts of one community group may inspire others.

An innovative and successful reading program started at one school may inspire other schools to participate, and reading scores across the district may improve. One person circulating a petition to "underground utility wires" may motivate a neighborhood to work together. Organizing a neighborhood cleanup of parks and streets may inspire others to become involved in the community.

If you wait for all the resources to be available before you tackle a problem you won't ever begin tackling the problem. Action itself begins the solution of the problem.

Optimism, hope, a desire to improve or to make things better are not catchwords. They embody what being in local office is all about. One of the major responsibilities of an elected official, and you won't find it in any official handbook or instruction guide, is to provide *hope*.

Hope inspires others; hope encourages people to get involved. If you have gotten to the point where you think problems are either too big to tackle or too insignificant to do something about, it is time to move on. If you have lost your optimism, lost hope, lost your desire to improve things, you should let others take your place.

Every elected official in our country will eventually leave office—all half a million of them. Unless they die in office, they will either leave office voluntarily or the voters will decide to retire them involuntarily. The only questions are, when will they leave and who will make the decision—the elected official or the electorate?

Early in the career of an elected official, before he or she becomes accustomed to the power and the responsibility of being in office, it is a good time to reflect on how much will be enough. One term? Two terms? Three terms? When will it be better to let someone else serve the community?

Was your goal to be a career politician? Do you need to be elected to feel important or to serve the community? What goals did you have when you were first elected? What else do you want to accomplish in the office you now have? Do you have ambition for another office? If so, what do you want to accomplish in that office?

While you may have had ambition for higher office, you never know if that will be an option. Opportunity and luck may determine whether that's feasible.

Moving on (a euphemism for leaving office) may be one of the most difficult decisions you face. On one hand, you have learned a lot in office and you have knowledge and experience that is valuable. You may be effective individually and as part of the group. You may find the work personally satisfying. You may feel there is a lot of work left to do. You will likely get a lot of pressure from colleagues and friends urging you to continue your public service.

On the other hand, you don't want to be considered a dinosaur or someone who has served too long. You may have already run for an additional term of office, even beyond what you initially felt was appropriate. You may also feel burned out. Leaving office and turning over decision making and power to others is rarely easy. The Roman Emperor Cincinnatus (our American city Cincinnati is named after him) is remembered not for the great deeds he accomplished as Roman emperor, but because he chose to leave power, voluntarily. George Washington, of course, set the standard and precedent for American presidents for 150 years by voluntarily stepping down after serving two terms.

At the local level, tradition and term limits may limit the number of years an elected official may serve. But even without term limits, most elected officials should leave office *before* they are ready, and while they are still effective. There will always be work left to do when you leave, or anyone else leaves, office. For every person that is still effective in office after several terms, there are many more that have stayed too long. Change is good.

New people bring new ideas and new energy to the job. Hopefully, you did. So will others. Yes, it will take some adjustment from the staff and other members of the elected board. A newly elected member will require that the other elected officials and staff adjust to the new team that now exists. This is a healthy process. Even in well-run public agencies entrenched leadership, like entrenched power, can breed conformity, mediocrity, and perhaps corruption.

Of all the reasons to stay in office, the most pathetic is "there is no one else." If this is true, and it rarely is, it is an indictment of you and your leadership. One of the responsibilities of leadership is to mentor others and to provide opportunities and training for others. Training and inspiring new leaders should be something you do from the beginning.

You got where you are, in part, due to the assistance of others. Make a practice of giving credit to up-and-comers and help them be successful. Allowing others to share the limelight is not only good politics, but it will breed better leaders who can follow you when it is time for you to move on.

During the course of your career, you will have countless opportunities to inspire and encourage good people to serve in an elected capacity. Every community needs people to serve on commissions and boards. Individuals who are involved in community organizing or school improvement efforts or who serve on community boards can make good elected leaders. All of these opportunities can be a training ground for the next generation of leaders. One of your most important responsibilities is to make sure others are prepared to serve after you.

Who are you mentoring? Who are you encouraging? Who has that spark, intelligence, or experience that would be valuable serving the public in office?

If you are not mentoring anyone, why not?

Another reason people stay too long in office is their fear of being irrelevant once they leave. After having calls promptly answered or returned, having personal staff (who are paid for by someone else), being introduced as "honorable" at community events, and being acknowledged as a leader in the community, it is hard to imagine a world where you are a regular Joe. A former office holder told me a few months after leaving office (in his case voluntarily) that it was difficult to get used to people not promptly returning his calls. Even at the local level, people get used to being in the limelight, and the transition back to normal life can feel empty.

It is natural to feel special when you are acknowledged as a leader of your community. Returning to private life can be a big change and hard to get used to.

Most people who retire have an exit plan. What is yours? What are you interested in that you can accomplish as a private citizen? You know, better than most, how important volunteers are to serve on boards and commissions. Have you considered serving in a volunteer capacity? Your leadership and experience could be invaluable to any number of organizations or causes.

Your knowledge of government could be useful, and not just as a lobbyist. Some communities have citizens' academies where community members learn about all aspects of city government to get a sense of what people do. Does your community have such an academy? If so, volunteer to teach. If not, establish one.

One former member of a board of education became a full-time housepainter and a part-time volunteer at an elementary school. She said she had tremendous satisfaction doing both jobs after her tenure on the school board. A former mayor became chancellor of the local community college. A person who served on a city council began a green technology start-up. A three-term incumbent opened a boutique chocolate factory, employing a number of inner-city youth. Another went back to school to earn a law degree and now is a city attorney in another community. A former mayor taught a class at the community college in civics. A former member of a hospital district volunteered to be the campaign chair to pass a bond to renovate the local public hospital.

The opportunities are endless and the need vast. Have you thought of what you want to do after leaving office? Now is a good time to start.

OTHER RESOURCES

Hollywood didn't make the sequel to *The Candidate*. Today, years later, we still wonder if Senator Bill McKay was successful in office. We can only guess. The thousands of citizens who are elected to office every year have a choice. They, like Bill McKay, can say "Now what?" or they can roll up their sleeves and begin to tackle the problems they were elected to solve. Here are a few resources that will help.

The chief executive of the organization is an excellent resource for newly elected public officials. Ask your city manager, superintendent, or chief administrator for recommendations on training sessions organized by local associations for newly elected public officials. If she or he has not conducted an orientation for new governance team members, ask for one. If you need to learn about a major policy area or issue, see if a special study session could be scheduled.

State and national associations provide useful guides and training to newly elected officials. The following organizations have a wealth of information and offer plenty of opportunities for elected public officials to learn:

- **California School Boards Association (CSBA)** is a member-driven association that supports the governance team, including school board members, superintendents, and senior administrative staff. The organization provides advocacy, policy analysis, training, and education for school districts and county offices of education. Go to their website for more information about CSBA's services and products: http://www.csba.org/. Information and education guides are available at http://connect.csba.org/store/, including a great guide, *Becoming a Better Board Member: A Guide to School Board Service* (http://connect.csba.org/store/p-30-becoming-a-better-board-member-a-guide-to-effective-school-board-service.aspx).

- **The Institute for Local Government** is the nonprofit research arm for the California State Association of Counties (CSAC) and League of California Cities (LCC). The institute has a growing list of resources to help newly elected officials understand both the substance and process of local governance. Their resources are available through the LCC's and CSAC's respective educational institutes for newly elected officials, and through the institute's informative website: http://www. ca-ilg.org/local-government-101. The institute also publishes a series of *Understanding the Basics of . . .* publications that explain the nuts and bolts of how local government works, land use planning, public service ethics, and where city and county revenues come from. They recently released *Financial Management for Local Officials: Questions to Ask,* available at http://www.ca-ilg.org/post/financial-management-elected-officials-questions-ask. Another "basics" guide on public engagement is in process, but in the meantime, check out the terrific resources available to local officials at http://www. ca-ilg.org/public-engagement-0. In addition, the institute has a publication on campaign ethics available at http://www. ca-ilg.org/taxonomy/term/754. All the resources the institute publishes go through a peer review process that helps the institute's publications reflect the collective wisdom of local officials.

- **National League of Cities (NLC)** is dedicated to helping city leaders build better communities. NLC offers training and education to local officials throughout the year: http://www. nlc.org/build-skills-networks/education-training. To learn more about locally organized citizens' academies, go to http:// www.nlc.org/home.

- **National School Boards Association (NSBA)** is a nonprofit organization representing state associations and member districts across the United States. Discover tools, publications,

191

activities, and other resources to strengthen boardsmanship skills: http://www.nsba.org/Board-Leadership/Governance/Policies.

The Internet provides amazingly easy access to a vast supply of online resources and written publications. Following are a few places to explore to get started:

- **Howto.gov** is a website to help government workers deliver a better customer experience to citizens. Learn about best practices and examples of how social media can be used in collaborative government: http://www.howto.gov/social-media/using-social-media.

- **The League of Women Voters** recommends effective ways to engage the public in a great resource guide: *Citizens Building Communities: The ABCs of Public Dialogue*, available at http://www.lwv.org/content/citizens-building-communities-abcs-public-dialogue.

- **PublicCEO.com** is a local government news site that provides a statewide perspective on California's cities, counties, and special districts. The site contains useful information on best practices in governance procedures: http://www.publicceo.com/.

- **John Carver** has published a number of informative books on board leadership and governance, including: *Boards That Make a Difference: A New Design for Leadership in Nonprofit and Public Organizations* (Jossey-Bass 1990; 2nd edition,

1997; 3rd edition, 2006). More information is at http://www.carvergovernance.com/pubs.htm.

- **Mary Jo Zenk** recently authored *The 7 Keys to Unlocking the Secrets of Your City's Budget.* You may download a copy at http://www.zenkconsulting.com/home.php.

Author Biography

Larry Tramutola is recognized as one of the country's top political strategists. Larry is an expert on grassroots organizing and political strategy, and is regarded as the country's top expert on passing difficult tax measures. Larry is an advisor to mayors and elected officials of all levels, and his list of clients includes school districts, community colleges, hospitals, healthcare organizations, cities, counties, and transit agencies.

Larry is the author of *Sidewalk Strategies*, which has been described as a "must read" for anyone involved in organizing or political campaigns. He directed the field operations in California in two presidential elections and was chosen to help train community leaders in South Africa in electoral organizing prior to that country's first free elections. He is the president of Tramutola | Advisors, one of California's most successful political strategy firms, and founder of TOLA, The Organizing and Leadership Academy.

He frequently serves as a facilitator at conferences for the California School Boards Association, the Association of California Healthcare Districts, California Special Districts Association, California Library Association, and the League of California Cities. Larry graduated with distinction from Stanford University and worked for eleven years as an organizer with Cesar Chavez and the UFW.

CPSIA information can be obtained at www.ICGtesting.com
Printed in the USA
LVOW07s1155250913

354057LV00004B/4/P